# Compassionate Fire

Fr. Robert Wild is a providential choice as editor of *Compassionate Fire*, the complete correspondence between Thomas Merton and Catherine de Hueck Doherty. With this book, we now have available both sides of their fascinating exchange of letters beginning with the early 1940s until Merton's tragic accidental death on December 10, 1968. It can be highly recommended to all seekers of the truth.

**Brother Patrick Hart, O.C.S.O.**
Abbey of Gethsemani

The letters of Catherine de Hueck Doherty and Thomas Merton show us in very human ways the struggle one must go through in order to live as an authentic Christian in the modern world. It is an excellent book that will inspire anyone who tries to understand their faith, will encourage anyone who tries to live their faith, and will guide anyone who desires to share their faith with others.

**Lorene Hanley Duquin**
Author of *They Called Her the Baroness: The Life of Catherine de Hueck Doherty*

The letters are an engrossing read of an intimate relationship between two people passionately in love with a God of justice and mercy. The early letters are especially interesting, as they express the deep influence that Catherine, through her work with the poor in Harlem, had on Merton during his initial years of discernment of his vocation. I knew Catherine in her last years, and experienced the strong spiritual presence she communicated with those on the journey. What is most striking in the letters is the intimate contact that persisted between the two of them through the years, as they continued to share a spiritual friendship that had developed out of a mutual love for the poor.

**Fr. Damien Thompson, O.C.S.O.**
Abbot Emeritus
Abbey of Gethsemani

Reading these letters is like listening to a conversation between two warning canaries in a dangerous mine shaft. Both Catherine Doherty and Thomas Merton were contemplatives and sensitive to the dangers facing the Church: faith being absorbed by culture, inattention of the clergy, the lure of wealth, and the neglect of the poor. It is not too late to pay attention to these letters and to be moved in faith to take our Catholic life seriously. To do this, however, we will have to follow their example by seeking God honestly, praying deeply and consistently, reflecting critically, and striving for a holiness that knows the demands of love.

**Fr. Francis Martin**
Professor of New Testament
Dominican House of Studies

The living testimony of two great souls aflame from the same Holy Spirit.

**Richard J. Payne**
Founding Editor-in-Chief, *The Classics of Western Spirituality*

# Compassionate Fire

The Letters *of*
Thomas Merton *&*
Catherine *de* Hueck Doherty

*edited by* Robert A. Wild

ave maria press AMP notre dame, indiana

Published by arrangement with Farrar, Straus and Giroux, LLC:
Excerpts from THE HIDDEN GROUND OF LOVE: THE LETTERS OF THOMAS MERTON
ON RELIGIOUS EXPERIENCE AND SOCIAL CONCERNS by Thomas Merton, edited by William H. Shannon. Copyright © 1985 by the Merton Legacy Trust.

Excerpts from THE SEVEN STOREY MOUNTAIN by Thomas Merton, copyright 1948 by Houghton Mifflin Harcourt Publishing Company and renewed 1976 by the Trustees of The Merton Legacy Trust, reprinted by permission of Houghton Mifflin Harcourt Publishing Company.

Excerpts from *The Secular Journal of Thomas Merton* by Thomas Merton copyright © 1959 by Madonna House. Reprinted by permission of Curtis Brown, Ltd.

---

Founded in 1865, Ave Maria Press is a ministry of the Indiana Province of Holy Cross.

www.avemariapress.com

ISBN-10 1-59471-216-6          ISBN-13 978-1-59471-216-6

Photograph of Thomas Merton by Sibylle Akers. Used with permission of the Merton Legacy Trust and the Thomas Merton Center at Bellarmine University.
Photograph of Catherine de Hueck Doherty used with permission of Madonna House.

Cover and text design by Brian C. Conley.

Printed and bound in the United States of America.

*Library of Congress Cataloging-in-Publication Data*

Compassionate fire : the letters of Thomas Merton and Catherine de Hueck Doherty / Robert A. Wild, editor.
    p. cm.
  "Introduction -- Letters: 1941/1949 -- Letters: 1950/1959 -- Letters: 1960/1968 -- Catherine's talk on the occasion of Merton's death -- Afterword.
  Includes bibliographical references.
  ISBN-13: 978-1-59471-216-6 (pbk.)
  ISBN-10: 1-59471-216-6 (pbk.)
  1. Merton, Thomas, 1915-1968--Correspondence. 2. Trappists--United States--Correspondence. 3. Doherty, Catherine de Hueck, 1896-1985--Correspondence. 4. Catholics--Correspondence. I. Wild, Robert A., 1936-
  BX4705.M542A4 2009
  282.092'2--dc22

2009015295

To the young man who wrote *The Seven Storey Mountain*,
the book that radically changed my life.
And to Catherine: she changed my life even more radically.

It has ever been a hobby of mine (unless it be a truism, not a hobby) that a man's life lies in his letters. So, not only for the interest of a biography, but for arriving at the inside of things, the publication of letters is the true method. Biographers varnish—assign motives, conjecture feelings—they interpret Lord Burleigh's nods, but contemporary letters are facts.

—Cardinal Newman, in a letter to his sister Jemima
May 1836

For nothing is more sacred than a letter or a conversation in which one human being opens his or her heart to another, who factually has no right (like a priest in confession) to that confidence. So it becomes at once both a tremendous privilege and a heavy, God-given responsibility.

—Catherine de Hueck to Thomas Merton
October 25, 1941

In October [1941] I was writing long letters, full of questions, to the Baroness, who was still in Canada—and getting letters just as long in return, full of her own vivid and energetic wisdom. It was good for me to get those letters. They were full of strong and definite encouragement.

—Thomas Merton
*The Seven Storey Mountain*

# Contents

# ACKNOWLEDGMENTS

Thanks to Brother Patrick Hart, O.C.S.O., for his help and for first suggesting this book; to Paul Pearson at the Merton Trust Center at Bellarmine College in Louisville, Kentucky, for his advice and encouragement; to Charles Skriner at Ave Maria Press for his editorial work on the manuscript; and to Farrar, Straus & Giroux for permission to reprint Merton's letters to Catherine, as edited by William H. Shannon in *The Hidden Ground of Love.*

# INTRODUCTION

It's an understatement to say that, at the present time, Catherine de Hueck Doherty is not as well known as Thomas Merton. In a letter to Fr. Louis (Merton's religious name), February 6, 1950, she says, referring to his quite prominent mention of her in his autobiography, "You have made me famous in a strange fashion." However, Catherine was not always less famous than Merton.

In 1941 "Tom," as she called him then, was hardly known at all to the public, and probably not at all in the Catholic world, whereas Catherine de Hueck had a fairly high profile in North America for her work with the poor in Canada and for interracial justice in Harlem. In the late 1930s, and throughout the 1940s, she was being invited to many parts of North America to speak about her work in Harlem.

Books about Merton abound, but there are relatively few about Catherine. My main interest in presenting their correspondence is to make their relationship better known. It's important to keep history alive. Most of my generation first heard about Catherine in that autobiography of Merton's, *The Seven Storey Mountain* (*SSM*), one of the most providential books of the twentieth century in America. The present younger generation may know something about Merton, less about Catherine, and probably nothing at all about their friendship. A few biographical details about them may be helpful.

Catherine was born in Russia in 1896. Raised in a deeply Christian Orthodox and fairly wealthy family, she had to flee the country with her husband during the Revolution. Making their way through Finland and England—where they entered the Catholic Church—the young couple arrived in Canada in 1921. During the Great Depression, Catherine opened soup kitchens and clothing rooms in several Canadian cities. She called this network Friendship House (FH). In 1938 she opened Friendship Houses in Harlem and other U.S. cities, concentrating especially on interracial justice.

In 1947 she returned to Canada to serve Christ in the rural apostolate in Combermere, Ontario. A group of laymen, laywomen, and priests joined her in this work. She called the new community Madonna House. Catherine died in 1985. She is probably best known for her books *Poustinia* and *The Gospel Without Compromise*. Her cause for canonization is in progress.

Thomas Merton was born in Prades, France, in 1915. After attending Cambridge University in England, he moved to New York to live with his grandparents, completing his education with an English degree at Columbia. He converted to Catholicism and taught English at St. Bonaventure University (at that time, St. Bonaventure College) in Olean, New York. He entered the Trappist Order at Gethsemani, Kentucky, in December 1941, taking the name of Louis; he was ordained a priest in 1948.

Merton wrote more than fifty books, two thousand poems, and numerous essays, reviews, and lectures. He died suddenly, being accidentally electrocuted by a malfunctioning fan in his room while he was attending his first international monastic conference near Bangkok, Thailand, in 1968. Through his writings, he is probably the most famous Catholic monk in the world.

Merton first met Catherine when she spoke at St. Bonaventure in 1941. He had heard about her work in Friendship House when he lived in New York City, but he had never met her. On that very evening, after hearing her powerful and inspiring talk, he was moved to ask if he could come to Harlem. (How many others had asked and had never come!) Catherine said yes. He spent "two weeks of evenings," as he put it, at Friendship House in Harlem. He met Catherine again later that same year at St. Bonaventure when she came for another talk.

For the rest of that year he struggled to discern whether he had a call to Friendship House or to the Trappists. It's significant that Merton trusted Catherine for discernment about his vocation. In his recently published unedited journal, *Run to the Mountain* (*RM*), he wrote: "It is beginning to seem that when the Baroness came and told me again to get out of here and come to Harlem, it was right, it was time for me to go. . . . If the Baroness came back and told me to stay, I'd stay, until somebody, who knew as much as she, came along with some other idea" (November 4, 1941, p. 451).

Thus, certainly in 1941, he owed Catherine encouragement and spiritual guidance at a time when he was really adrift and without too much clarity as to what his next vocational step should be.

In a talk at the University of Memphis, June 8, 2007, Jim Forest said about Merton: "When the Franciscans turned him away due to his checkered past, his next vocational attraction was to be part of a community of hospitality. People like Catherine de Hueck Doherty and Dorothy Day inspired him. He found it extremely difficult to choose between Friendship House and the Abbey of Gethsemani—between a life shaped by the works of mercy and a life centered in prayer."

It may be of interest to point out a few common themes in their thinking and spirituality. Not being a Merton scholar—but perhaps a mini Catherine scholar—I will confine myself to several of the themes that are expressed in these letters. Indeed, since both wrote prodigiously, a comparative study of their spiritualities would make a good book.

There is a passage from *Run to the Mountain*, November 29, 1941, that succinctly contains the several themes I will briefly consider here. It is a significant passage in that the intensification and importance of the gospel values Merton mentions in this passage flow directly from his experience of Catherine's gospel way of life in Harlem. Catherine's witness and apostolate revealed to him the kind of gospel life he wanted to live.

> There is no question I can't stay at Saint Bonaventure any more: I must go and find Christ where He really is—in real poverty and real sacrifice. . . . But then, what about Friendship House: it has this one great thing: it is real poverty, it is real sacrifice; it is real love of Christ in the poor. It is holy. The work is holy. The Baroness is a saint. Harlem is full of saints. And in Harlem there is no doubt a possibility even of martyrdom, in which my sins would all vanish at once and I would be certain of pleasing God, and coming to Him as His child, spotless, clean and holy and a saint! (*RM*, p. 464)

Harlem was one of the places where he could give everything to God: "After all, there are certain points where the crisis is acute, and there the Christian is called to be—one is the cloister, the other, Harlem, any slum" (*RM*, p. 466).

I will reserve the most important theme mentioned here—holiness—for my afterword, since it forms the heart of the question I ask there: "What did Merton *owe* to Catherine?" I treat briefly here the theme of real poverty, and add two others: the importance of silence and solitude for the modern world ("cloister"), and writing as an apostolate for the Church. This last was not central for Merton in 1941 as he was seeking his vocation, but writing was a gift that both he and Catherine would dedicate to the fostering of the kingdom.

Real poverty was one of Merton's desires, as he wrote to Catherine:

> When you came along, everything you said made perfect good sense, and I was glad to think that perhaps this was what I had been praying for. I saw FH, and liked it: what actually inspired me was the idea of complete, *real* poverty, without security. (p. 21)

> He lives in us, and through our poverty He must reign. And I need not tell you how poor He makes us in order to reign in us. If we knew how poor and desolate we would have to be when we begin to follow Him, perhaps we would have fallen back. (p. 35)

Catherine had a passion for personal poverty, and a realization of the special presence of Christ in the poor. As a very young girl in Russia she used to go with her mother "into the people" as part of a movement among the wealthy to bridge the gap between the rich and poor. But it was in the lives of Christ and St. Francis that she saw identification with the poor as an ideal for the Christian life. In Harlem, Merton witnessed her joy and spirit of adventure in such a way of life.

With regard to solitude and silence, as Merton was moving towards solitude and the hermetical life later on in his own monastic vocation, he was very enthusiastic when Catherine told him of her introduction of the *poustinia* into North America. Catherine is probably best known worldwide for her book *Poustinia.* A tradition from Holy Russia, a poustinia (desert) was a cabin where a person lived a life of solitude, prayer, and penance. It was a sort of "hospitable" approach to the desert: the person was available for visits, and for helping with the manual work needs of the community.

In 1962, Catherine introduced this tradition in Combermere, mostly to pray for the ongoing Second Vatican Council. But we now have on our grounds in Combermere twenty or thirty such cabins, and many members of the community often spend a day there in prayer, solitude, and penance. Catherine wrote Merton about this new venture. He replied:

I was deeply moved by the Poustinia project. That is ideal. It is just right. It will be a wonderful contribution. It is the kind of thing that is most needed. And though it is certain that we must speak if and when we can, silence is always more important. The crises of the age are so enormous and the mystery of evil so unfathomable: the action of well-meaning men is so absurd and tends so much to contribute to the very evils it tries to overcome: all these things should show us that the real way is prayer, and penance, and closeness to God in poverty and solitude. (November 12, 1962, p. 72).

Merton's many writings about silence and solitude are well known. He had some longings to be a Carthusian; eventually he got permission to be a hermit on the grounds of Gethsemani, a significant development in the community-centered spirituality of the Cistercians.

At the close of her talk to the community at Combermere upon Merton's death, Catherine said: "There are some very beautiful passages about many things in our letters. We corresponded through the years. You know that he was seeking a poustinia. Finally his superior allowed him to live in one. He was so happy about that."

In my correspondence with Brother Patrick Hart, a monk of Gethsemani who served as Merton's secretary in the final year of Merton's life, in the course of compiling this book, I wrote: "I think Merton would have liked the book *Poustinia*, don't you?" (It wasn't published until 1975, seven years after Merton's death.) He replied: "Yes, I think Louie would have loved *Poustinia*, since it was, in a way, a response to something of his writings on the contemplative life for lay people, and not just something for monks and nuns."

Catherine, during all her apostolic life, saw writing as one important form of the apostolate. She was ecstatic when, after starting her own apostolate, she came across Dorothy Day's *Catholic Worker*.[1] It inspired her to start her own social action newspaper, *The Social Forum*. She had a newspaper in Harlem, and then in Combermere. Currently she has over twenty books in print. She married a newspaperman, the journalist Eddie Doherty. One of the most interesting things that I found in these letters is her early encouragement of Merton to write. He probably would have gone on to become a great writer without Catherine's encouragement, but I'd like to think she gave him a good push when he was starting to doubt his talents! In one such passage, Catherine reassures Merton that his writing is not a form of pride:

Pride? No, that is strange. I would never have associated pride with you. If writing is your vocation, go ahead and write. But always with a prayer in your heart and diffidence in your soul, for a written word is such a potent weapon for evil and good. There cannot be any connection between talent of any sort and pride. Real talent is very humble because it knows its origin, and also its terrific burden. For each talent received, one has to render an account. And such a gift as writing or painting, why, that is 100 talents, and hence a hundred in return. (October 14, 1941, p. 11).

Limiting the play of my imagination as much as possible, I will now simply let the letters speak for themselves—the "facts" of their relationship, as Cardinal Newman said, the "inside" of them. When Merton finally decided upon the Trappists, Catherine was one of the first persons to whom he wrote of his decision:

I entered the community as a postulant this afternoon. After that it will no doubt be hard, but at least I will know there is nothing keeping me from God any more—I can belong entirely to Him by simply consenting to each trial as it presents itself, and that is enough! It is everything. I only want to belong entirely to Him. I will never forget FH in my prayers! And pray for me! And write, sometime! Merry Christmas. (December 13, 1941, p. 26)

They would never meet again, but they did "write sometime."

# I. LETTERS: 1941–49

## Thomas Merton to Catherine de Hueck

St. Bonaventure College

*October 6, 1941*

Dear Baroness and everybody else,

First, thanks very much for letting me stand around Friendship House for a couple of weeks of evenings: I hope I can do that more often. I liked most of all the clothing room, but wasn't there much. I think the "cubs" are certainly very smart fine kids, and think about them a lot . . .

You will be interested in this one: I have a nun in a freshman English class (one from the kitchen here—the only nun I've got in regular classes for this year), and she wrote an essay about St. Bonaventure in which she listed all the things that had impressed her since she had first come here. Baroness de Hueck was outstanding on this list: the sister was very impressed with what you said, and although she didn't go into details, evidently agrees with you. Well, I nearly gave her an A on the strength of this, but I didn't. Charity is one thing: art another. In heaven they are identical, on earth too often distinct. A for charity, B-plus for technique was what I gave the sister, only the first grade remained unspoken, and that was just as well too, because today she gave me a big argument about some obscure point of grammar.

For a couple of minutes I talked to a Quaker woman who was passing through here. She had spent the summer in Kansas working among Negro sharecroppers, not without some guarded hostility on the part of the local authorities. She had with her a lot of students from Allegheny College, Meadville. I talked of you and Friendship House and got a smarter and more enthusiastic reaction than you get from the average Catholic . . .

Right now besides my work I am doing a lot of reading and studying and meditation, and a little writing but nothing systematic, just notes on what I am thinking about, when I am thinking about anything that doesn't look disgusting as soon as it gets on paper.

Mostly it has something to do, in general, with the question of lay vocations, both in an academic sense and in a personal one too. The academic sense is maybe more interesting. There is one problem about lay vocations that interests me a lot, and it is obviously very important to Friendship

House too: except that you probably have it all doped out to your satisfaction. I haven't yet. The problem is this: where does Catholic Action stop and politics begin?[2]

First of all, it seems to me that you yourself illustrate the proper balance between them. That is: Catholic Action, which is another word for Charity, that is Love, means, for one thing, feeding the poor, clothing the needy, and after that, saving souls. A person who is really interested in that must also necessarily be interested in certain political movements which tend to help feed the poor, clothe the needy, etc. Also, a person who is charitable, and really loves the poor, realizes just how little pure political action, without any charity behind it, really means.

If you make laws to provide the nation with old age pensions and the nation is populated by people who beat up their grandmothers, your old age pension law doesn't mean much.

If you make a law (and this time nobody is being funny) providing the unemployed with unemployment insurance, and then refuse to employ certain classes, or types, or races of people in any decent job, your law is never going to eliminate unemployment . . .

When you get down to it, Catholic Action means not voting for anybody but going out and being a saint, not writing editorials in magazines, even, but first of all being a saint.

I said it was a problem. In any place where people are engaged in doing things, as you are at Friendship House, for the love of the poor and, through them, God, there isn't much of a problem. Where it comes in with me is trying to explain guys like Franco, or some of the Medieval Popes, in whom Catholic Action (or what they imagined to be that) got totally submerged in a completely materialistic and political struggle between certain social and political groups. The problem I am getting at is, is it possible for there to be a completely Catholic government? Is there any point in these Catholic political parties, like the ones that used to exist in Germany and Italy? and so on.

If a Catholic gets into a position of power in a country where the political atmosphere is made up of struggles between a lot of irreligious and frankly selfish minorities, how can he ever do anything at all except by compromising with religious principles, or, worse than that, fooling himself that he is leading a crusade, and then turning the country upside down in the name of religion, the way Franco did, or the way the Third and Fourth Crusades did to Europe. I think the Reformation was a divine punishment for the Fourth Crusade, in which the businessmen of Venice inveigled the whole army of Crusaders (recruited with promises of plenary indulgences if they died in battle) to conquer, for Venetian business, the Christian empire at Constantinople!

On the other hand, I believe there is only one free and just state in the world, and that is the Vatican City: but that is less a state than a glorified monastery. Now assuming all the people in a given country were good Catholics, it might be possible for that country to be ruled the way the Vatican City is ruled: that is, politics would be, all down the line, subordinated to salvation, and ordered to the salvation of souls as its ultimate end. Then you would have real freedom, real justice, and everything else.

Which brings us back to the same conclusion: the first thing to do is to feed the poor and save the souls of men, and in this sense, feeding the poor means feeding them not by law (which doesn't do a damn bit of good), but first of all at the cost of our own appetites, and with our own hands, and for the love of God. In that case, feeding the poor and saving them are all part of the same thing, the love of our neighbor . . .

And when it comes to saving souls, once again writing and talking and teaching come *after* works of love and sanctity and charity, not before. And the first thing of all is our own sanctification, which was the lesson I got out of my retreat at the Trappists [in Holy Week, 1941] and keep finding out over and over again every day . . .

If I can only make myself little enough to gain graces to work out my sanctification, enough to keep out of hell and make up for everything unpleasant, in time, the lay vocation, as far as I'm concerned, presents no further problems, because I trust God will put in my way ten million occasions for doing acts of charity and if I am smart maybe I can catch seventeen of them, in a lifetime, before they get past my big dumb face.

At this point I realize that this letter is disordered and obscure and badly written and probably extremely uninteresting to everybody. But even if it doesn't make sense, the very fact that I used up so many words talking about lay vocations and writing means that I think I am finding out something about writing and about the lay vocation for me: which is that my vocation is probably to go on finding out this same thing about writing over and over as long as I live: when you are writing about God, or talking about Him, you are doing something you were created to do, even if you don't feel like a prince every minute you are doing it, in the end it turns out to be right: but when you are writing or talking about some matter or pride or envy to advance your own self, you feel lousy while you are doing it and worse afterwards and ten times worse when you read the stuff over a week later . . .

Meanwhile, I hope you will come up here again and make some more speeches. The seminarians could do with some ideas about Harlem. I understand the clerics (who have now long ago returned to Washington) are still in a ferment. I'm going to write to one of them and find out, anyway. By the time I get to writing to him, I will probably have thought up another dull and complicated treatise instead of a letter!

But I think a lot of Harlem, and I'll tell you the one reason why: because Harlem is the one place where I have ever been within three feet of anyone who is authentically said to have seen visions—what was the old lady's name? I have forgotten. But believe me when the angels and saints appear among us they don't appear in rich men's houses, and the place I want to be is somewhere where the angels are not only present but even sometimes visible: that is slums, or Trappist monasteries, or where there are children, or where there is one guy starving himself in a desert for sorrow and shame at the sins and injustice of the world. In comparison with all these, St. Bonaventure occasionally takes on the aspects of a respectable golf club, but then again I won't say that either, because the place is, in spite of everything, holy, and when you live under the same roof as the Blessed Sacrament there is no need to go outside looking for anything . . .

This letter is being written not according to plan, but according to the clock, and now it is time for me to wind up and turn in. Maybe you are lucky. But anyway, God bless everybody in Friendship House and in Harlem and hear all your prayers, and please pray sometimes for us here . . .

Tom Merton

## Catherine de Hueck to Thomas Merton

Pax

*October 14, 1941*

Dear Tom,

Your letter of October 6th was a little gem all its own. I did enjoy its rambling ways, and here is an attempt to answer some of the portentous questions you raise. You will have to forgive my typing. It is rotten, to say the least, but here goes.

It is we of FH that really owe you a vote of gratitude for coming to FH. You were of more help than you ever will suspect. God bless you, dear friend. Yes, the Clothing Room is interesting, though one hardly can call "interesting" the laying naked of human need, the opening of a social ulcer of such magnitude, that it crushes you to watch the operation.

The Clothing Room is a very hard place to be in. One has to have nerves of steel to behold man's inhumanity to man—all day, every week of the year, and bow before it helplessly. We apply only palliatives to the vast problem of the Naked Christ. For what is the use, one thinks at times, of writing, lecturing, and speaking on ideals and principles, primary or secondary, of Christianity, of Society, of Finance and social works and set ups, when millions of people in the heat and cold of the day stand patiently before many such Clothing Rooms as ours, waiting to be given a dress, a coat, that has already been worn by the more fortunate ones of this world long enough to be stretched at the seams.

In this affair one of the primary human rights is being challenged. Therein is proof positive that even such simple truths as the fundamental rights of men to food and shelter and clothing are not met in our modern "progressive" and tragically inadequate civilization. But from the point of view of the cold-headed scientist in social problems, the Clothing Room is interesting.

The Cubs? Yes, they are interesting too, and fairly smart kids if by smart you mean the worldly, and almost bordering on lawlessness, smart. The Cubs to me are such a source of sorrow and pain that I rarely speak of them at all. These little children are the Magnifying Mirror of what Harlem really is. They do not know what a clean wholesome home is like. They never or seldom have seen God's green earth and its fruits and flowers. Their main job is to survive amidst the filth and immorality of Harlem, and they become tough as leather. Evil is their constant companion. And when it does not get hold of them it is a miracle, and a first class one at that.

Such words as discipline (self or otherwise), fair play, sportsmanship, etc., are not in their vocabulary. And for each of those little and precious souls God died. And look what we whites and society in general is doing to them!!!!! No wonder there are Hitlers in this world today. God often allows events to take their course, and faces man with the net result of his follies. The year of grace 1941 is such a "result."

How very nice of the darling Sister, but it really wasn't the Baroness. What good ever comes from my lectures is the great miracle of the Holy Ghost using this poor inadequate instrument that is I. Yet I am glad that she liked me, because what I had to say had to be said, and damn the consequences. Yet, it is a gift that some of them are bearing fruit. Too bad the A was not forthcoming.

Yes, in Fr. Hubert you people have a giant.[3] I hope you know it. I also hope that chemistry, or whatever he is teaching, is not going to make him hide his spiritual light under a bushel. He is too big, I guess, to do that. By the way, tell him when you see him that he owes me a letter. His letters are like a breath of fresh air in an atmosphere heavy with storms. Tom, I am getting more frightened by the minute about USA Catholics. They are the ones I know best. What, oh what, is going to wake them up to the fact that in their sinful hands they hold the heart of the world, ITS LIGHT AND SALVATION, but that the only way to teach it is by example?

The Quaker Woman is typical. I speak a lot at the Protestant places and always find them wide awake and raring to go. How tragic that so much good will and energy is often taking the wrong turn.

My spiritual director has advised the same program to me. He wants me to leave the details of FH to the crowd whom he knows and considers ready for the responsibilities of running the FH daily routine. And I am to pray more, meditate more, and write down everything I think of—when I am thinking—even if it looks disgusting on paper and send it on to him, which is what I am trying to put into being now. So I know, in a small way, just how you feel. Yet prayer and meditation are such a great help. I meditate best in writing, by the way. And already I have about 18–20 thick exercises books on my meditations. One thing I am glad about is that they never shall see the light of day.

Ah, here you touch me to the quick: LAY VOCATIONS. That is my dream, my goal, my whole hope. Do not misunderstand me, I am all for the religious vocations, especially that of the priesthood. I think they are the crux, the nucleus, of the Church's life. But on lay vocations I am on fire. For don't you see that that is the only way to leaven the masses. The "Comrades" have the right idea there. A select few Comosols just turn the rest of the Community inside out with their enthusiasm and their ability to carry on in the face of all obstacles and opposition. Think of what WE CATHOLICS could do if we took our lay vocation seriously, and started with daily mass and communion. Lord have mercy on us for not seeing that the two last Popes have been killing themselves, calling in season and out of it for just that sort of a vocation.

Academically one could write books and books on it. Factually and actually, it is the most adventurous, exciting thing going. But you wonder how to reconcile politics and lay vocations. That question has been thrashed out in Belgium re the Jocists and by the Cardinal Patriarch of Lisbon when I interviewed him.[4] May I rather clumsily and condescendingly give it to you!

First, Catholic Action is never political action. The Catholic Actioneer, the cell, the heart of the members of that movement, the inside ring, as it were, of leaders, never take part in political action. They indoctrinate others as to the primary principles that govern clean Christian political ways and workings. But since the leader is also a person and lives in a State, in a country, he in turn must apply to himself his indoctrination.

Example.

The Jocists were the first leaders in Belgian Catholic Action. At the same time they were workers in factories. So, when conditions in one factory became intolerable, they AS WORKERS struck. But while they were striking as workers, they applied to themselves all the Catholic principles of a just strike. The same applies to voting.

Summing up: a Catholic Leader of Catholic Action takes part in political action when it concerns him as a person or individual, in the legal meaning of the word "person." But he does not take part in such political movements that are not a matter of his personal relationship with society. He indoctrinates others—lawyers, politicians, heads of States, capitalists and labour, judges and doctors, generals and privates—on their conduct and principles in the matter. Get the point? Have I made myself clear?

For, like all vocations, the lay vocation will develop into what one could call, for lack of a better simile, choir people and lay religious, the Marys of the movement, and the Marthas. And then there will always be with us the multitudes that will follow the leaders. I hope that is clear. Ask me more questions if it is not.

Now, regarding the interesting part of the whole question. Undoubtedly you are right there. Anyone interested in the question of, say, helping the poor, naturally is interested in the laws that help them. But here comes the rub. One must not be doing the political angle, or getting mixed up in the promulgation of laws, except when one has to pass or vote on them as a "person." What one does is to try to get ever higher in Catholic Action, and arrive, at long last, at the very centre of the laity, of the law, that makes and works on them.

Somehow, as I write, I understand that it gets complicated, and more so by the minute. But remember the Pope's words—Catholic Action by the people in their own circles—worker to worker, and so on. Well, there you have the answer: lawyer to lawyer, and statesman to statesman. Get the idea? But he who is the focus of the radiation of Catholic Action does not indulge in political action, except as a person. That is the axiom laid out by the late Pope in 1933.

The next paragraphs of your letter really are touching on the inner core of the whole problem; and here is the answer as I see it. Catholic Action starts with YOURSELF. You have only one person to REFORM, and that is *you*. Then enters the supernatural, to which you haven't allotted any place in your arguments as far as I can see. When one does work on oneself first, with only one thought in mind—to love God and save one's own soul (remember that one cannot prove one's love for God unless one loves one's neighbor)—well, then, God enters into the picture and somehow brings other souls to you. And you become a leader. (Leadership is never acquired or imposed. It is conferred by the group on one person whom they really feel and think can help them.) I am now speaking of Catholic and spiritual leadership in Catholic Action only. That is why I am opposed to "schools or courses" for leadership. Taking a course in it DOES NOT MAKE ONE A LEADER. But reforming oneself for the love of God and neighbor, and for the salvation of one's soul, DOES often make you a chosen leader.

Once this is so, a group is formed mostly thru the effects of the Holy Ghost, first on one individual, and on others who have been led to the first, then group action begins. And here the concentration at first (and always) is on the simple and primary teachings of Christ. After a while the group itself will select and apply these teachings, first, academically, then factually, to their lives, be they politicians or Negroes. That is how it works in reality.

But the leader must never lose track of first things first: to be and not to do, is the primary maxim; then, to beware of the heresies of good works. Again: first to LOVE GOD AND KNOW HIM. Out of this follows much prayer, thought, meditation and then action. Don't you see how that works? If you behold the fullness of GOD'S TRUTH thru the Blessed Sacrament, then all your work gets into the right proportion, and instead of being a simple intellectual with knowledge in width, you now become a Christian intellectual with knowledge in DEPTH.

Out of this comes the right results in the line of politics, and so on. Yes, it means a Saint, or trying to become one. Yet, it also means teaching others politics, writing for magazines, speaking and teaching, because a Saint (as all things of God) is a well-rounded person, ready and able to do what God wants him to do. And that might be some or all of the above. Charity is simply part and parcel of the Saint because its other name is LOVE. And one cannot be a Saint and wield the above weapons unless that foundation is ready. But never separate sainthood from ordinary living. For, after all, what is it fundamentally but doing everyday things extremely well.

What makes you say that Franco was doing Catholic Action, or any of the Popes were doing Catholic Action? What passed for Catholic Action then was a sop to the people to swallow so that the bitter medicine of the political ambition and greed of the leader would not appear so terrific. Or perhaps, to be more charitable, it was a hope of these leaders to placate God with little bribes. I agreed fully on your definition of the Reformation —God's mills grind slowly but exceedingly small.

The Vatican might be a just state, but it cannot today be a model because the ways of living there are no pattern to the outside world. No clerically predominating group can be a model for lay people. Their vocations are different, and hence the pattern is different. Portugal is more of an example. Read up on it if you haven't. Salazar has the goods there.[5]

The first thing to do is to start with oneself; then the rest will come.

Here in the USA the problem is immense. Neither laws or politics are important here. Only one thing matters—to bring out from the dust of years CHRISTIANITY, and show the people its workings which is the face of Christ in the hearts of men. And that is for the time being the duty of a handful of people. Here is where Friendship House and the Catholic Worker come in. They are and exist primarily to awaken people—Roman Catholics at that—to their obligations, by assuming, in a spectacular manner, the corporal and spiritual works of mercy; and using all the means of propaganda [news] papers, lecture platforms, writing, and above all, living, to bring forth these forgotten fundamental truths. Do you think we would seek publicity as we do unless it was for that reason? Like Simon Stylite astounded people (pagans) and made them curious to know why he stayed on his colonnade, so we make people curious as to why we are in HARLEM, or Little Italy. To each century its own technique.

As to nightmares and the like, well, there are several explanations of the same. One is the mystery of iniquity which is as great and as potent and mysterious as that of the good. Then there is the way Christ lived, and the shadow of the cross; and the Easter way only being reached thru Calvary; and deeper still the blinding light of God shines best on the stygian darkness of the world. And so down the line. It is a great question that needs hours in answering.

Go and stand up and tell everybody the tiniest bit of truth God has sent you. You must, for if that grain is to grow in the hidden soil of souls, you have to plant it. To you God has given a little bit of it. But what you plant in another soul he will water; and how do you know if that will not grow into a mighty tree. Go ahead and tell loudly and clearly and never mind the laughs that hurt. Keep on!

Pride? No, that is strange. I would never have associated pride with you. If writing is your vocation, go ahead and write. But always with a prayer in your heart and diffidence in your soul, for a written word is such a potent weapon for evil and good. There cannot be any connection between talent of any sort and pride. Real talent is very humble because it knows its origin, and also its terrific burden. For each talent received, one has to render an account. And such a gift as writing or painting, why, that is 100 talents, and hence a hundred in return.

Yes, the second kind of writing is the best. Its roots are in God not the devil. The other argumentative kind is a waste of time, and dangerous, unless done under orders [obedience].

Yes, again, you've got what it takes. You have the right approach. The shaft of God's light is striking you straight in the face. For a while you are a little blinded by it, but soon you will learn to see fully in his light. And then, Tom, oh Tom, you will become so very small that your writing will be like fire; and like sparks of the Holy Ghost, lighting little torches everywhere to illuminate our terrific modern darkness. Do pray so very hard now. That is the way to write these fiery, startling words. Communion, Mass, and prayer, and you will get there.

Mary Jerdo does want these articles.[6] Why not write one [titled] "Why I like Harlem." The lady's name, by the way, is Chambers; and visions are the least of her sanctity. Pain is the greatest test. Lots of it borne uncomplainingly and beautifully. She is dying of cancer of the intestines.

St. Bonaventure is a respectable golf club where quite a few saints have lost themselves on its greens. Some day it is going to change all the golfers into saints. I like it. It has undercurrents that are good and very strong. It will awaken fully some day. Watch and see. I have to finish this now. It is more disjointed than yours. Yet, off it goes. Hope you'll answer it soon. Say a whispered prayer to our Lord for me.

Affectionately. B

## Catherine de Hueck to Thomas Merton

*At the beginning of the second letter of Merton's (p.18), dated November 10, 1941, he says he sent two letters to Catherine while she was in Canada. Unfortunately, these two letters have not been preserved. In this next letter of Catherine's, she is answering one of those two lost letters. Thus, some of the references here are not able to be explained.*

*October 25, 1941*

Dear Tom,

Not having a coat I cannot strip it to answer yours. Thanks, though, for the compliment of liking my letter. I write like I speak, from the heart and the mind. Sometimes that gets me into deep trouble. But, as you say, it is worth it. There is something about a piece of white paper that just calls out to one, especially if one's correspondent is as congenial as you are; and as full of desire to know and to spend himself, both for the ultimate purpose of better serving God and men.

Time, what is time? It is a precious commodity to be sure to be used for God, because He will ask an account of us for each second of it. But once in a while, when writing to someone like you, or praying, etc., or talking to the poor, time is of no importance because it is then occupied with the things of eternity. At that particular instance it projects itself into eternity, and is pleasing to God, and a joy to one who spends it thus, as it was to me when I wrote to you.

Yes and no. I both know how hard it is to get a letter back like that, and also no, I don't, for as you say, I seem to be that sort of a person people both write and talk to freely. I am always awed by that grace of God, for that is a great grace; and it would be foolish of me or you to deny it. But, nevertheless, it is a gift that I for one treat reverently. For nothing is more sacred than a letter or a conversation in which one human being opens his or her heart to another, who factually has no right (like a priest in confession) to that confidence. So it becomes at once both a tremendous privilege and a heavy, God-given responsibility. I treat it as such, and beg him for light on my answers. For in the first place it was He who directed that letter or conversation to me. Don't you feel the same way?

Yes, that is also one of the many things "that dazzles me silly too." It is marvelous to see the workings of God's grace in the midst of that sink of iniquity that is the modern world, to see that beauty in the midst of our abomination of desolation. I agree with you, too, that it was a part of Bloy's vocation, and in a sense a very great, burdensome and heavy part. I wonder if he realized it as fully as he—with all his lights—should have. Sometimes, I think he did, and then again I think he did not.

Lord, how you went and frightened me. I write my meditations; I write 9,000 letters a year; I have established a lengthy correspondence with at least a hundred priests; and God alone knows how many laity; even a Bishop figures on the list. And you mean to tell me that they might not destroy my letters, and that all this accumulated material will some day see the light of day! God help us—me, I mean. For alas, dear Tom, far from showing a staggering, beautiful though tragic picture of a vocation, they will show up all my weaknesses, foibles, vices and faults. Oh, I am not saying I can't write a letter; that would be foolish. I can, but I hope truly and earnestly that they will not be preserved for posterity, and I mean this.

And why should you be cute about it! There is in you a hidden vitality that I felt, a hunger that stretches out—even to me—for knowledge and inner knowledge. There is a fire that burns under your easy-going and smiling exterior. There is what it takes there, and much of it. So, God who fashioned you uses you to help others. And at the same time it is as if he allowed you the greatest gift, the lifting of the veil that separates us normally from Him. You have felt that, haven't you, each time you meet someone that talks to you about God? Never mind if it is for or against Him, for he whoever bothers about God one way or another is hearing the baying of the hound of heaven.

But when you read or speak to people, doesn't it happen to you, as if, little by little, thru each person, there comes to you a new aspect of God's face, like pieces of a puzzle that you reverently and with fear put together, and with awe notice that it begins to look like his likeness? Each of us contributes to the other's knowledge of God; but sometimes it is so sharp, so etched out, that one almost wants to close one's eyes. Yet, do not be astonished that it happens to you. You have fulfilled the first part of His commandment: You have arisen and started on that journey that seeks a goal—Him. And you have begun to go on that road that will eventually lead you to sell all to buy that pearl of great price.

So, because of that, people are already coming to you. Take them simply, as you do, reverently, as you should, and lift them, and yourself thru them, ever higher and higher toward Him who has been lifted up to draw all things to Himself.

About writing. Go ahead and write articles and books and everything; but here is the way I see it: write for the simple, the unlearned, the unproud. Write for the lowly and the humble, and for those who spell badly, and for those who hold a magazine clumsily. They are so hungry for knowledge, especially of God, that you and I look like overfed spiritual bourgeois next to them with all our fire and hunger for divine things. Write for them, and the learned will come to you, and the wise will listen to you, and the proud will bow to you. And God will smile on you.

Oh, how I wish I could explain my idea that we should write for the masses, taking the place of the Communists who write a catechism of dialectical materialism so that a two-year-old can understand. Look how God spoke: the Gospels are the gem of human literature even though they were all directed to tailors and fishermen and house wives.

We do not write great things and truths simply enough. We forget that greatness is best naked and blunt, and not all dressed up in highfaluting words of skyscraper vocabulary. That is what is the matter with us. And so we have no readers. People outside are hungry for the same idea expressed simply in one syllable words, or sentences. I am so hipped on that idea, I am just rampant.

Ah, the war, the terrible war that maims bodies and souls, and raises question after question; and has no answer in her thunderous noise of planes and bombs. Their very noise shutting out answers, and God. And yet Kilmer saw God in the War, and He is there, everywhere where His children suffer and die and are sick.[7] Yes, the war is bound up with all our lives; and what is still stranger, bound up with a lot of lives yet unborn. Only the dead have peace.

And then again, behold the WAR. You and I, and Tom and Dick and Harry and Jean and all us little folks, we made it, we watered it with our selfishness, that seed of greed and indifference that we have been planting since the Reformation, and lately since Versailles. Behold the handiwork of our hands. Surely this war is you and you it; and it is all woven in your history and life and mine and everyone else's. We begot it out of the bowels, not of compassion, but of miserliness. Remember the depression? We gave that dime for a cup of coffee alright, but shamefacedly, and with nothing of charity. And what is more, we never gave *ourselves* with it.

Look at the Negro and Harlem. That is the field that is being labouriously tilled by us and made fertile for the revolution to come. And when it will come, we will sit academically and discuss the horrors of it, our allegiance with this and that branch of it, utterly unaware of the simple fact that WE were the instigators of it as much by the things we DID NOT DO as by those we did badly.

So no wonder the virus is everywhere, because the cause and the fault, the sins of omission and commission, are everywhere. Wars are always evil, and this one is no exception. And what makes me glad about your letter is that you speak of prayer and penance in relation to it. I am so sick and tired of "America First" and their opposition shouting their big mouths off for this or that side. All sides are suffering, and the Mystical Body is crucified everywhere.

And what we Catholics should be doing is penance and prayer and more penance and ever more prayer. But instead we create a war within a war by our arguments and discussions. One does not discuss much when one is drowning. One prays. Oh, Tom, when, when are we going to know and do first things first? Tell me!

I have read *A Thousand Shall Fall*, and many more like it.[8] The horror of it is still with me. I have gone through a War, a Revolution, and the stench of human blood is forever with me. And I know what men in machines that fly the skies can do to men without any that walk the earth. And I know, first hand, of children and women dying from hunger. The sight is ever before my eyes, and driving me like one possessed, to keep the eyes of others clear from tears, to keep the arms of other mothers cradled about their babies, to keep other human beings in the midst of plenty in the City of New York away from starvation. The war is only, in a way, the intensification on a grand scale, of what has been going on in our city. The bullets of gangsters no older than the Nazis have killed thousands, and cars driven by drunken fools have killed millions. And the people of Belgium are dying for want of bread, and so are Negroes; as well as the poor in the north and south of the USA.

Yes, in the USA they have thousands of gods, just as you mentioned. It is like the many-handed and many-faced Hindu gods. Many yet one. COMFORT, that is the first child of the bourgeois spirit. And there we are. So what, I could ask cynically. But tears are in my eyes and I cannot be cynical.

Facing the facts, I would go and fight because by doing so I would not be sinning. But at least I would offer myself in intention as a victim of expiation for my sins against my brethren. There are sins, you know, that can only be washed in and by blood given freely in reparation. I am now in Canada, a country at war. And here, too, every rule and law that touches the comforts of living is met by arguments, with pros and cons which, summed up, means, "Let someone else fight this out, but do not touch my ice cream and radio. I have to listen to the ball games, you big bully." Sacrifice is a word that just isn't in the modern vocabulary, until the bombers come and spell it out, I guess.

Your paragraph on the Mystical Body and Communion came as a breath of fresh air after the fetid discussion on selfishness and greed. That is just it: You can help others to infinite life. And that is the crux of the whole thing. That is why Harlem to me is paradise, because I can help to infinite life too. That is all.

I love St. Therese for the greatness of her little way. We strive for big things, and she, at 20, knew that neither "big" nor "little" mattered: only God's will is abandonment personified. For the past 15 years I have struggled to conquer myself and learn that hard and simple virtue. He is always somewhere around, showing me how. I got the cheque, and I will not thank you for it: I will thank God that He made you see things in their right proportion. That cheque will be a great thing for you. It will reach God's hands and repose there for eternity. Someday, you and He will face each other and He will open that hand. Perhaps, at that moment, it will seem blank to you, and the check will flutter to your feet and you will hear GOD SAY: THANK YOU—and then you will know what BLISS is.

In Him, Catherine

## Thomas Merton to Catherine de Hueck

*November 10, 1941*

Dear Baroness,

. . . I feel rather astonished, to begin with, at the subtle way you interpreted the big fanfare of speculation that came along with each one of those two letters I sent to Canada, because, when I wrote them, I was deliberately steering clear of anything that might be interpreted as having anything to do with vocation . . . So when you started out, in the car, while we were riding back from Buffalo, by saying that any person who asked all those questions probably wanted to be a priest, you (1) surprised me, (2) woke me up to the fact that maybe I am very bad at being abstract about anything, (3) you scared me. The priest business is something I am supposed to be all through and done with. I nearly entered the Franciscans. There was a very good reason why I didn't, and now I am convinced that Order is not for me and never was. So that settles that vocation.

Meanwhile, about being at St. Bonaventure: that's easy. I cannot even give myself half an argument that this is the place for me to stay. From the moment I first came here, I have always believed nothing about the place except that, for me, it was strictly temporary. It is not enough. There is something lacking, for me. I have plenty of time to write, and that has been nice, I am sure. The teaching is like a sort of harmless hobby: about on the plane of stamp collecting. In any visible results it may have, as regards the Kingdom of God, it is just about as valuable as stamp collecting, too. But of course this is only my second year. And besides, visible results aren't much, and it is a kind of weakness to strain your eyes looking for the results that men are capable of seeing on earth . . .

I don't know what it is that will help me to serve God better: but whatever it is, it doesn't seem to be here. Something is missing. Whenever I read about the young rich man in the Gospels, who asked the Lord what he should do, beyond keeping the Commandments, and turned away, sad, "because he had great possessions," I feel terrible. I haven't got great possessions, but I have a job, and this ease here, this safety, and some money in the bank and a pile of books and some small stocks my grandfather left me, nothing that the average housemaid or A & P clerk doesn't have, in good times. But I don't feel comfortable at all when I think of that sentence in the Bible. I can't read that and sit still. It makes me very unquiet.

And then when I am filled with that unquietness, I have learned at last that the only thing that will take it away again is to go down into the church and try to tell God that everything I have, I give up to Him, and beg Him to show me how He wants me to give it to Him, in what way, through whom?

Just before you came down here, and I wasn't really thinking of Friendship House at all, I had been saying that prayer and finally started a novena to find out how to give God what He was asking of me: thinking all the time of possessions: maybe some poor person would be brought to my knowledge and I could give him something of what I have received through God's goodness.

So then you turned up. If you are surprised that I gave you one feeble argument and then shut up, that is why. Not that I wouldn't, in ordinary circumstances, be so full of arguments I couldn't even see straight. But in this case it was altogether too clear for argument, nor have I been able to work up even the slightest interest in any argument against leaving here since you have left . . .

However, at least by God's grace I know what to pray for harder and harder every day. Nothing but the strength of His Love, to make me love to deny my fears every time they come up. A nice high ideal. The very thought of how I have always been, under difficulties, makes me so ashamed there is nothing more to do but shut up.

Also, there is this.

I don't know if you are concerned about the past of people who come to work for you. I am bringing this up because it might possibly be important. I got in some trouble once, which I don't particularly want to tell anybody about. If you absolutely want to know, I will tell you, but otherwise I can say in good conscience that I don't believe, myself, that it would disqualify me from working in Friendship House, or bring any scandal to be connected with FH in any way, or reflect on you or anybody else, nor is it anything that makes me in any way different from anybody else, but once I did get in some trouble, enough for it to be an impediment to my becoming a *priest*. I repeat, to the best of my knowledge it does not in any way affect my fitness to work at Friendship House. On the other hand, it is something that definitely demands a whole life of penance and absolute self-sacrifice: so that if I thought the Trappists would take me, I think I would want to go to them. But I have to do penance, and if Harlem won't have me, then where may I turn?

If I had never mentioned this, I am sure that it never would have come up in any other way, and I am sure it could not possibly be dragged up out of the past, because it remains only something between me and God and the other persons involved, with whom I have unfortunately lost all contact: or so it seems. Maybe it would have been better to have ignored the whole thing.

However, it came up and spoiled my last "vocation" [see *SSM*, pp. 296–98], and I don't want to leave anything in the background to spoil this one. I assure you that it is something which, if the president of this college knew, I don't think he would fire me for. I just got a sudden attack of scruples, maybe, when I brought it up.

But if you have any doubts at all, say so, and I will tell you the whole story, in which I am no white-haired hero, no model of self-sacrifice or of holiness either.

The general burden of this letter is to let you know that, in me, you are getting no bargain, and I feel I should especially tell you this, because you have done me an inestimably great honor, far above my own worthlessness, in asking me to come to FH, even before I got around to asking it myself. I believe that, since with God all things are possible, with His help I can some day be a Saint, if I pray without ceasing and give myself totally to Him. In all this, I depend on a miracle: but His grace is always a miracle. Apart from that miracle, however, there is the present fact that I am not only not a Saint but just a weak, proud, self-centered little guy, interested in writing, who wants to belong to God, and who, incidentally, was once in a scandal that can be called public, since it involved lawyers.[9] So that's the dirt. Never forget me in your prayers!

Yours in Christ, Tom

## Thomas Merton to Catherine de Hueck

*In this letter, Merton is replying to a letter of Catherine's "from Chicago"—her reply to his letter of November 10, 1941 (pp. 18–20). Unfortunately, Catherine's Chicago letter has not been preserved.*

*December 6, 1941*

Dear B,

Many thanks for your fine letter from Chicago. I feel very guilty for bringing up all that business while you had so many other things to worry about, especially since certain things have occurred since then that make it seem pretty definitely that I am not to have the privilege of trying a year or two at FH.

But the problem I felt I had to put before you had been bothering me so much: and the fact I brought it up shows that; and also, it finally led me to do something I ought to have done long ago.

You see, I have always wanted to be a priest—that is, ever since my conversion. When someone told me that there was an impediment against my ever being ordained, I was very unhappy, and really, since then, I had been really quite lost, in a way. I knew I wanted to belong to God entirely, but there didn't seem to be any way particularly suited to fill up everything in me that I had hoped would be filled by the priesthood. I tried to get as close to it as possible by coming to Bona's and living just like the priests here, under the same roof as the Blessed Sacrament: but the work itself didn't seem to mean an awful lot, and everything seemed to be a little dead. I simply stayed here, praying and waiting to be shown what I was to do.

When you came along, everything you said made perfect good sense, and I was glad to think that perhaps this was what I had been praying for. I saw FH, and liked it: what actually inspired me was the idea of complete poverty, *real* poverty, without security: and also the fact that Harlem is where Christ is, where the Blessed Mother is more likely to appear than anywhere—except perhaps, a Trappist monastery! As to the actual routine of work, I can't say it meant any more to me than St. Bonaventure and teaching. I like teaching . . . But always it would seem to me like marking time, like waiting for something else, filling in an interval.

Meanwhile I had made a couple of Trappist retreats, and was practically driven silly by the conflict between my desire to share that kind of life and my belief that it was absolutely impossible. Of course, the obvious thing to do was to ask somebody else about this impediment: whether it was really as serious as I had been told.

There were two reasons why I hesitated. First, I had been told it was a total, complete, irrevocable impediment in such strong terms that it seemed fantastic even to question them. Second, the devil made use of this to try and kid me that all this thinking about a religious vocation was just a silly, dramatic self-indulgence, and that I would never really be able to stand up under the life, in actuality, and that I had best forget all about it. Well, I could not forget about it, but I stalled around, having argued myself into such a state that it was almost impossible to do anything: and all along I had been *arguing* with myself instead of praying, which of course didn't help matters, but definitely guaranteed that I would end up in what you refer to as a "pretzel": and what a pretzel! A regular Gordian knot of a pretzel I was in!

Well, when I had agreed to go to Harlem, it seemed as though the question was answered, for the time being. I could try Harlem, and if the question came up again, well, then I could see about it then.

Then I made Father Furfey's retreat.[10] His retreat was all about Harlem and nothing about Trappists, except that it dealt with the one infinite source of life that nourishes both Friendship House and the Trappists, the Mystical Body of Christ: but all from the point of view of the former. It was a terrific retreat, and I came back here all on fire with it.

And what happened? I started thinking about the Trappists again. This time, I was in such a pretzel that it was evident there was no use fooling any more, the question had to be settled. This time I didn't argue, I prayed, and the most apparent thing after that was the desire to question this impediment, and question it with every question I knew how. In short, I went to one of the priests here, who ought to know, and he told me at once that in his opinion there *was no* impediment and never had been. He was so definite, in his turn, that it knocked me flat. I rushed out of the room saying all I could remember of the *Te Deum* and went and fell on my face in the chapel and began to pray and beg and implore Almighty God to let me be admitted to the Trappists as a choir religious.

So then I wrote to the Trappists, simply saying I was coming for a retreat, and, this was in line with the priest's directions: I intended to ask for admission then, nothing about it in the letter. Of course, it *might* possibly happen that the retreat would change my mind (which just seems absurd) and then I would return to the idea of Harlem. What is much more likely, it might happen that the Trappists would not have me anyway. Then, again, I would know I should try Harlem for a while. But anyway, I was now getting to some definite answer to all my problems.

A few days later, another thing happened, that now rules out Harlem for good.

All this time I had been assuming that the classification 1B I got from the Draft Board last spring was going to be definite for a while. However, they now want to reclassify me; and if they make me 1A I am liable to be sent off at once. What is going to happen about *that* is still unknown. It is all in God's hands. I have asked for three months, to find out whether or not the Trappists will take me. I still don't know whether the Draft Board will give me that time, or merely drag me into the army without any more speech. All I can do is pray, and wait patiently to do God's will, meanwhile begging Him with every breath that He may forgive me for resisting my vocation so long, and may now, in His infinite bounty, let me be accepted into the cloister, not by reason of any merit in me, but only because of His goodness.

That is what has been happening. So you see, it is apparently not God's will that I should serve Him in Harlem now. Needless to say, all this has felt like being ground between two millstones, but one thing is more and more clear each time the stones go round: I don't desire *anything* in the world, not writing, not teaching, not any kind of consolation or outward activity: I simply long with my whole existence to be completely consecrated to God in every gesture, every breath and every movement of my body and mind, to the exclusion of absolutely everything except Him: and the way I desire this, by His grace, is the way it is among the Trappists. FH made sense to me, but I was not eaten up with this kind of longing for the lay apostolate that I seem to have for a contemplative community and a life of prayer and penance. Only these things and the thought of them makes me live, interiorly, now. Everything else actually seems not only dry, but painful: but the thought, and fact of prayer and fasting are totally sweet and peaceful. Never forget me in your prayers, B., especially now. I am unshakably rooted in faith in this vocation: but there is the army [that] may try to kill it in me. So pray for me! My love to everybody. Bob Lax wants to be a staff worker: he is a very good guy.[11]

P. S. Remember me especially between the 14th and 20th when I expect to be down at Gethsemani, Kentucky, trying to be admitted!

Tom Merton

## Catherine de Hueck to Thomas Merton

Friendship House
34 West 135th Street
New York, NY

December 13, 1941

Dear Tom,

Your letter was awaiting me upon my return. It would be foolish for me to say that I wasn't disappointed, and yet how could I be? If the retreat of Father Furfey brought to your mind the Trappists, then probably it is the will of God.

I do understand perfectly, dear Friend, and though in these hard times F.H. seems somehow to me to be the front line of the spiritual and moral front of all our conflict and we propose to stick to it through thick and thin; nevertheless, I understand. When I say that, in my heart a Te Deum and Magnificat are singing for you. Deo Gratias.

How wonderful, how perfect! A Trappist and a priest! High is your calling, dear friend, and wonderful to behold the Face of God in silence. It is awesome and ever so consoling.

Let me know when you are going and how things are shaping [up]. If you are going to be here for Christmas, drop in and let us have a chat and God be with you as well as my poor and humble prayers.

Write to me.

Affectionately, Catherine de Hueck

P.S. How about that car. Are we getting it, or not. If we are, I do wish it would come because it is so important just now.

## Thomas Merton to Catherine de Hueck

Abbey of Gethsemani, Trappist, Kentucky

*December 13, 1941*

I entered the community as a postulant this afternoon. After that it will no doubt be hard, but at least I will know there is nothing keeping me from God any more—I can belong entirely to Him by simply consenting to each trial as it presents itself, and that is enough! It is everything. I only want to belong entirely to Him. I will never forget FH in my prayers! And pray for me! And write, sometime! Merry Christmas.

## Thomas Merton to Catherine de Hueck Doherty

*In 1948* The Seven Storey Mountain *was published. It became a national bestseller and brought fame to its monk-author.*

*February 14, 1949*

After all these years I have an excuse to say hello and ask your prayers. The excuse is this. A lady in California thought, for some reason, that she ought to give away seventy copies of *The Seven Storey Mountain,* a book I wrote, for people to read. My job was to get them distributed. Friendship House in New York distributed twenty, and forty more went to prisons, and I thought you would be able to handle six. I am also sending one to you personally in case you have not read it. Not that it is so wonderful.

But I would be very grateful if you could handle this for us. As you know, out here we are not in touch with spots where these things would do the most good.

In the last seven years I have found out somewhat of what God wants to do with people, and what His love means. When I say this life is wonderful it doesn't mean that every other vocation isn't wonderful too: but to be in the sort of place where God wants one: that is certainly a marvelous thing. As soon as you get set in your groove, boy do things happen!

People still accuse me of being enthusiastic, but I guess I am a little saner than I used to be? Anyway it is good to be quiet enough to let God work and not get too much in His way with one's own pep, because when my own steam obscures everything things don't move nearly as fast.

It seems funny to talk about things moving in a place where nothing ever happens. But more has happened here in seven years than I would have imagined could happen anywhere else in seven centuries. And yet, on the surface, nothing has happened. Somewhere in it all there have been a lot of prayers for you and for Friendship House and I know I have been getting a lot in return. In fact now that I have written a book, I am being prayed for much more than I have prayed for others and this reversal of the usual situation for a Trappist is disconcerting. But it is also very nice, because I sure feel the benefit of those prayers. Maybe I can store some up for the future . . . But if I can't I'll take it out in trust.

This is my first chance to say how happy I was to hear of your marriage [to Eddie Doherty in 1943] and to send you congratulations and best wishes and blessings. I can see where being married can bring those whose vocation it is much closer to God. Also it is good to hear, once in a while, that Friendship House is branching out here and there.

We read your book on FH in the refectory and it made a big impression, and I read *Dear Bishop* and thought it packed a great big punch. I hope it has done some good. But I can guess what kind of letters you got. I got one or two myself. Including one priest who flattered me by saying he didn't like me any more than he liked you. So we are sitting in the same boat. Let us pray that it may speed us to heaven with a million or two Americans for our companions and crown, something to give to Our Lord. His Providence certainly designed a rough age for us to be saints in.

So let us pray that we will get there: or you, who are on the way, pray for me who have been seven years starting and not getting very far. But I like it anyway.

fr. m. Louis (Tom Merton)

# II. LETTERS: 1950–59

*Catherine de Hueck Doherty to Thomas Merton*

*February 6, 1950*

Dear Father Louis,

This letter is one of a beggar, asking alms from you, the alms of prayer for my new book. It is coming out this year, published by Bruce [Publishing Company]. It is again a series of "letters," this time to Seminarians. It will be called *Dear Seminarian,* but it is really written to priests. And I am a wee bit afraid, not because it may not be well received—it probably won't be—not because I may have to be hurt again: I am used to pain, God's greatest gift to His friend. No. Lady Pain and I are old friends. No, I am a wee bit afraid of my temerity, for who am I to address myself to priests, to tell them what to do and how to do it? And yet, I HAD to write that book. It was in me to come out and so it came out. Pray, therefore, that it may be blessed by the Holy Ghost to whom I turned for every sentence in that book. Pray that it may do good to those to whom it is addressed. Thank you.

I am also finishing another book, *My Russian Yesterdays.* A series of "vignettes" on Catholic life in old Russia, showing the deep roots of faith in the hearts of my people. To help USA Catholics to understand Russians better.

And then, Father, I am starting on what I hope will be my last book, and this too recommended to your holy prayers. I have just begun it. It is a hard book to write but it too clamors in my soul to be written. I call it—to myself—*Journey Inward.* It is an impersonal book. It deals with the soul of a Catholic who has arisen thru the grace of God—it may be any Catholic—in search of God, and then started on the only journey worth traveling, "The Journey Inward," to find, to meet the God, the triune God, that dwells in his soul.

It is also the story of a Lay Apostle, the story of a slow stripping of self, to follow naked the naked Christ. A story of a man's (woman's) passion because his soul had fallen utterly in love with Love.

It is the story, too, that in some manner, yet unexpressed by words, but somehow familiar to me, of the ascent of one unto the path, the mountain, of prayer. The Lay Apostolate too is based fundamentally on contemplation and on living continually in the presence of God. So, in a manner of speaking, it is or will be the story of prayer.

You see why I ask you who know so much about the passion, about prayer, whose life is a prayer, to pray that I might have—may find—the words to express this book, to give it birth. For there is in me a drive, a compulsion, to write it, that is akin to a woman with child, knowing her time is nigh.

Forgive this somewhat "selfish" letter. I should, and want to ask, how you are. Somehow I know all is well with you. It seems foolish to say that daily I pray for you, but I do. Pray that nothing would ever distract you from prayer, from love.

You have made me famous in a strange fashion. *I* know it is because of your great charity, because in the great holy silence of God, caritas fills your soul.

I thank you for that great charity, and I will not bother you with an essay (which I could easily write) under the title of "The Woman Who Knew Tom Merton." I am afraid that it would be a humorous one that would bring too much laughter, worldly laughter at that, into the holy walls of Gethsemani. But maybe some day I will, for after all, laughter is the song of joy you live in, at least part of it.

FH is doing fine. A new one is opening, I hope soon, in Indianapolis, and in our new "FH Canadian Province." Signs indicate we may have a second one in Montreal, and that will be 8, if this happens. 6 now. We have invitations from Indo China, Brazil, Chile, for new foundations. Fancy that!

I saw Bob Lax's cousin in New London, Connecticut. Oh, pray for him. He is so close yet so far from the Church. He knows you, he says.

Forgive this long wordy letter, but I write to you seldom, knowing you wish it so, knowing too that in the Lord there is little need for words. But these books are on my mind. I need your holy help. I need—they need—your prayers.

In Him, sincerely, Catherine "B"

*Thomas Merton to Catherine de Hueck Doherty*

*February 13, 1950*

Dear B,

I was certainly glad to hear of those 4 books. They are around here, and I'll keep praying at Mass. It was good to hear of the spread of F.H. May God bless everything that you touch and everything that you do for His glory. May you spread His peace in souls and live deep in His Heart. And pray for me.

Fr. M. Louis, O.C.S.O.

## Catherine de Hueck Doherty to Thomas Merton

*At the time of this letter, Madonna House was seeking Secular Institute status from Rome. It never was approved as such. Madonna House was erected as a diocesan pious union in 1960 by the Bishop of Pembroke, Ontario. Also, in this letter Catherine raises the topic of a manuscript of Merton's that he left in her possession in 1941 when he decided to enter the monastery of Gethsemani, with the understanding that all rights to the manuscript belonged to her and that any proceeds from the publication of the manuscript would be hers to use in support of her work. The manuscript consisted of selections from a journal Merton kept between 1939 and 1941. As we shall see in the letters to follow, in their efforts to publish the manuscript, Catherine and Merton encountered some difficulties with Merton's Trappist censors. Originally called the* Cuban Journal, *the book was eventually published under the title* The Secular Journal of Thomas Merton *in 1959.*

*August 17, 1956*

Dear Father Louis,

It is such a joy to me that there is really a valid reason for me to write to you. Though I know that I could write anytime, I do not avail myself of this privilege often. First, because I know that there is no need of letters between us, because we are together in the heart of Christ. I know you are praying for us, and I know that you know that I am praying for you always. What could a letter add to that unity of prayer and charity? Moreover, there is also the human joy of communicating with a beloved friend when God allows it to happen. So let me really begin this business letter with an immense thank you for your kindness, courtesy and interest in the manuscript that you have left me so generously when you departed from Friendship House on your great adventure with God.

Naomi keeps me posted on all the developments.[12] I realize that you understand how tremendous the gift of that journal has now become, since your books have achieved fame even in the world.

Naomi writes me that she needs a written statement to prove that you have really given me that manuscript long ago and far away. So would it be possible for you to write me a letter so stating? I would appreciate it very much. I discover that there is so much red tape attached to these things.

This magnificent gift from you comes just at a wonderful time, when the constitutions of our Secular Institute of *Domus Dominae* (lay people) and *Domus Domini* (priests) have been approved by our Ordinary and sent for final approbation to the Holy See. (Ours is a Secular Institute of Priests, Men and Women.) The Holy Ghost literally seems to cover us with the full approval of His crimson wings, sending us many vocations of gallant young people wishing to dedicate their whole life under the three vows to the grueling work of the Market Place. (We also have already three priests in our ranks.) Bishops from Nigeria, Chile, Japan, Brazil, Glasgow, Scotland, Arizona, New Mexico, Yukon, and far and distant places are writing in for foundations.

The money will come in so handy for the simple primitive buildings that we need to house the many who come, and to help the poor who press around me like an ever-mounting tide.

Eddie and I have taken the three vows too. How good God is to us! It is unbelievable!

In His Infinite Charity and in His Beloved Mother, Yours affectionately, Catherine Doherty

## Thomas Merton to Catherine de Hueck Doherty

*August 22, 1956*

Dear B,

. . . I am so glad we are getting around to the publication of that ancient, prehistoric *Journal.* But I am especially glad that it keeps me in your growing spiritual family. I am a member of Domus Domini, at least by virtue of a manuscript which works for you in my place. I hope you will let me know the details of what is growing into a firmly established institute . . .

Now, as always, God's real work remains obscure and humble in the eyes of the world. Now more than ever, we have to be suspicious of results that are achieved by the efficient, over-efficient technological means of which the world is so proud. Christ works always humbly and almost in the dark, but never more than now . . .

Nothing is more important than prayer and union with God, no matter where we may be. Christ is the source and the only source of charity and spiritual life. We can do nothing without Him and His Spirit, and I know you are now, as always, seeking no other Mover than the Spirit of Christ. That is why the Cross will cast its shadow, still, over your life. But then, in that shadow, you will see the Light of Christ, the Light of the Resurrection. He lives in us, and through our poverty He must reign. And I need not tell you how poor He makes us in order to reign in us. If we knew how poor and desolate we would have to be when we begin to follow Him, perhaps we would have fallen back.

Thus we are left as children, as the saved remnant which is forgotten, we are like the animals in Noah's ark, which floats off on the waves of the deluge of materialism without anyone but God knowing where we will end up.

We have got to be people of hope, and to be so we have to see clearly how true it is that the hopes of a materialistic culture are the worst form of despair. We have to build a new world, and yet resist the world while representing Christ in the midst of it. I have been taken to task for yelling so loud that this is a perverse generation and no doubt I have put a lot of my own frustration into the cries: the people of the generation are good, so good, so helpless, some of them: the culture, the generation, is perverse and I see little hope for it. Why? Because by its very essence it is against Christ. I hope that I am wrong.

In the end, no theory that neglects real people can be of any value. It is in those that He sends to you that you see Him and love Him, and there you have a reality which cannot be taken away, a treasure like the one for which St. Lawrence died on the gridiron. You have Christ . . .

With all affection in Jesus and Our Mother, Fr. M. Louis (Tom Merton)

*Catherine de Hueck Doherty to Thomas Merton*

*September 3, 1956*

Dear Fr. Louis,

Thank you so very, very much for sending me that official release [for the publication of the manuscript]. It will do the trick with the publishers, indeed it will! I have made your letter my meditation for the time being. What I took to heart so much from it was "our poverty."

Yes, how infinitely poor we are, but also how rich in His grace and in His love.

I have felt very close to you in the past year. I think I have written to you once about it—that we often meet, I think, in the night. In the night of God. In the night of men. And in the natural night that covers our earth after sundown. My prayers are always with you, and I know that you are a member of *Domus Domini,* but not only via the MS that is going to work for us.

Affectionately yours in Mary, Catherine

*Thomas Merton to Catherine de Hueck Doherty*

*December 28, 1957*

Dear Catherine,

We have all been waiting a long time for the final judgment of the censors of the Order as to the publication of the *Cuban Journal.* Naomi Burton may have told you that it finally got to a fourth censor and the score, at the close of the thirteenth-inning, was three against publication and one in favor. There are apparently to be no more innings after that. In other words the Order is officially and definitely against. So much so that the Abbot General has written me a very long letter to this effect, instructing me as to the attitude which I myself am to take in the matter. He tells me that he feels it is my duty, in the circumstances, to ask you if you would consider forgoing your right to publish the book. In other words, while you do in fact retain the right to publish the book if you want to, he asks you in charity to take into consideration the feelings of the Order in the matter. He is concerned above all with passages which he feels would shock certain readers coming from a priest, a member of this Order, and the effect of the shock would make itself felt in a harmful way, he believes.

My position is such that in practice I have no choice but to conform to these wishes of my Highest Superior (below the Pope), and hence I have to communicate these wishes to you as my own. I am very sorry to have to do so. But, knowing that you, as well as I, will be disposed to see the whole business in the light of faith, and to accept the judgment of those higher up in the Church as God's will for us—always remembering of course that *you* haven't made any vow of obedience to my Superior, and you remain free to do what you want. I think we can certainly differ, privately and speculatively, with this opinion of censors who may not be blessed with a superabundance of judgment in such matters. Yet at the same time, they have reasons of a different order, and I think it would be rash for us to ignore these altogether. Incidentally there was no question of anything definitely against faith or morals, just the general tone of carping criticism of "nice" people, which they think is undesirable in one of my present status. Maybe so. It certainly is somewhat adolescent, and I thought the preface took sufficient account of this fact. They did not agree.

If you are still very anxious to publish the book, the only hope I can offer is the vague possibility that they *might* consent after abundant cuttings—but perhaps the cutting would be so abundant that the bulk of the book would be gone. My own opinion is that we ought to just drop the idea for the moment, and if God wills, we will have another chance some time later on.

So you see, the Cistercians of the Strict Observance are very much opposed to any voice with even a slightly radical sound being raised in their midst. I do not know whether or not I feel this is something for which we ought to be proud. However, every Order has its own spirit, and our General has been clamping down on all expressions of anything, on the rather reasonable theory that the monks came to the monastery in the first place to shut up. I cannot deny the validity of the argument. Father Abbot tells me that there was a $500 advance on the ms. and that we will take care of that, so that at least you will have got something out of the transaction.

I was happy to have a few words with Eddie [Doherty] when he was down here . . .

as ever, devotedly in Our Lord, fr. m. Louis

## Catherine de Hueck Doherty to Thomas Merton

*January 18, 1958*

Dearest Father Louie,

Your faithful letter of December 28th reached me a few days late. I would be a liar if I said that I was not disappointed. From the natural point of view, it was sort of a body-blow to the few little dreams—or were they big ones—that I permitted myself once in a while to dream about when I prayed, or thought, about the *Cuban Journal.*

They were dreams in the Lord, as usual. I have dreamt so many foolish dreams in Him, that I guess I acquired the habit of doing so. The more so that I myself could never tell if they were foolish or wise. For He would take some of them, as you well know, and make them come true; others He would leave lying around-about. Where? I don't know. But I imagine He must have a place for such dreams.

I dreamt of finishing some very humble—but, oh, some very vitally necessary—buildings at Madonna House. For our Lady and her Divine Son keep sending us vocations to this apostolate in the Market Place of ours. (This year we have 14 new Staff Worker Applicants—Novices!) I dreamt about another car that would take our nurses further into the snowy bush where so many poor farmers and their families live in tar paper shacks. And that would take ever more teams into the same bush to teach catechism to children who live too far away for our small group of nuns, and our over-worked parish priests to reach. This latter dream the pastor shared with me so much.

I dreamt if the sale of the *Cuban Journal* was successful enough to give a share of that money to a little hard-working farming family I know—who had so much bad luck lately—and to whom $500 would be equivalent to one million.

I guess I do not need to tell YOU, who for a little while shared Harlem with us, the funny little dreams that I once in a while allowed myself to dream when thinking of the *Cuban Journal.* You know them.

But the voice of your Superior has spoken. To me it means that I have to gather all these dreams, and lift them up into the hands of Christ, and add to them the strange heartache that I feel at the decision of your

Superiors. Foolish feminine tears come close to my eyelids, but I do not want to shed them, for the will of God is my sanctification too.

I will add to these dreams also, sinner that I am, a little strange sense of rebellion that I first felt when I read your letter. I am not so sure that I should put into the hands of Christ the violent temptation that assailed me, and with which I wrestled a whole day, of just going ahead and publishing the *Journal* and let the pieces fall where they may! But since I conquered the temptation, I guess I can add that too: the Lord can change it into something acceptable to Himself and use it some place else. But don't let me fool you, it was a big temptation. And I did wrestle with it, like Jacob wrestled with the Angel, though I am no angel myself.

And so, dear Father Louie, dear Tom, as I think of you often under that name too—and pray for you under both—you have my decision. I shall wrap up the original copy of the *Cuban Journal* [and send it to you]. I love to call it the *Journal for Catherine,* the title you so kindly suggested it should be named when the matter was first discussed in what now seems to be the long ago.

I guess obedience—yours anyhow—embraces in truth "shutting up," inside and outside. Since, in my estimation, obedience is the crown of poverty and the footstool of charity, I better be a good footstool to my favorite virtue, and get rid of, along with the foolish dreams, any critical attitude that my intelligence could develop *ad infinitum.*

So let's you and me, Father Louie, fold the wings of our intellect and close the door on manuscripts and dreams. Who knows but the Lord will open another door that neither you nor I know anything about.

Fiat.

You are in my humble poor little prayers daily. Strange as it might seem, you are closer to me as time goes by than you ever were in FH. You do not know it, but I talk to you often. In fact, I have written you many letters in my mind. For often I want to share with you many things, show you some others, and ask your advice about this or that. Some day you will read those letters, or better even still, we will discuss them together when we sit at the feet of God.

Now don't forget: pray that I might get there, and I confess that I want you to pray that I get there on a non-stop express ticket to heaven, that bypasses Purgatory. Somehow I have great faith in your holy prayers.

I will remember your special intentions—very especially, in fact. I have been doing that already, ever since I got your letter.

Please express my deep appreciation to the Superiors of your Order for that gift of $500 to us, which was, as you so well put it, a God-send to us.

In the infinite caritas of our Lady and her holy silence, I remain, yours lovingly, Catherine

## Thomas Merton to Catherine de Hueck Doherty

*February 11, 1958*

Dear Catherine,

Today we are celebrating the hundredth anniversary of Lourdes, and part of the celebration, for me, is to send you a piece of good news. It shows that Our Lady is with us, and that there is still a very solid hope that the *Secular Journal* (*Cuban Journal*) will be published after all.

Yesterday afternoon I heard from the Abbot General again. I had written him a letter after receiving your humble acceptance of his demands about the book. I explained to him simply that I still wondered if we were entitled to deprive your cause of such an important source of support. Previously he had shown himself opposed to the publication of the book *even if* I made the changes suggested by the censors. Now however I repeated the plea that at least I might be allowed to make those changes and submit the book once more.

Father General agreed to this, and expressed himself very content with the way both you and I had acted, and promised to reconsider the whole thing after the corrections had been made. The book will start off again to the two censors (or two out of that group of four) after I have made the corrections . . . I am sorry to have to mutilate it a bit, but perhaps it is just as well. My plan at present is simply to cut, not to change or rewrite if I can help it. However, it may turn out that some passages could be kept with a little rewriting, and if that seems to be so, I will try my hand at it.

There is one consolation in all this: I don't feel that the book is of such a nature that it has to be preserved intact the way it was written. I mean, it is not the same kind of document as the *Autobiography* of the Little Flower and nothing much depends on the fact that it may have been changed here and there, since in this case the changes may well be for the better. I wasn't a saint when I wrote the book, and I am probably still less a saint now, not that anyone knows anything about who is or who isn't a saint. Because all, even the saints, are sinners—except, as today reminds us, Our Lady.

The emendation of the *Secular Journal* might well be a matter of suppressing material that is sinful, offensive against charity perhaps.

If that is true, then the job will be a welcome one. Pray in any case that I do it the way the Holy Spirit wants it to be done.

I am happy to have this chance to wish you joy on Our Lady's feast.

Now, most important of all. I will have to write a new preface, and this will give me an opportunity to talk about Madonna Villa and all that it stands for and all you are trying to do. Please send me all the material possible, so that I can get a good clear idea of what is going on. I didn't even know until recently that you and Friendship House had parted company. Tell me all about the Institute (?), how you stand, what are your rules, etc. What is the official title again??? (Do you think it is smart to have an official name in Latin?) (Or don't you have an equivalent in English?) . . .

with all affection in Christ Our Lord, Tom/ fr. m. Louis

*Catherine de Hueck Doherty to Thomas Merton*

*February 17, 1958*

Dear Father Louie,

Frankly, I read the first paragraph of your letter and felt slightly weak. It is no use denying that I felt the weight of the choice very much. Yet, all along, as I read your previous letter, I knew that there was no choice. First, because it was the will of your Superiors; and though it didn't bind me in justice, it certainly bound me in charity. And then again, loving you, I didn't want even a little shadow to fall on you in anyone's mind because of your generous gift long ago and far away, even though I knew that you were used to more than shadows. You were acquainted with darkness itself, from whence such shadows come. But that made my empathy greater, because I too have known darkness, that very same darkness I speak about.

And now, on the feast of our Lady, there was your letter. It was a little difficult to adjust oneself to the idea, but I managed.

With you, I believe that our Lady wants this book published, for reasons all of her own. If I may very humbly express an opinion: so many people walk in those shadows that your superiors are afraid of, that our Lady probably knows how much a book by you, who knows the road out of them so well, will help others.

Whatever her reasons may be, I thank her for this next possibility, this other chance.

Well, I don't know. It certainly isn't the autobiography of the Little Flower. And you may not be a saint now. But who can tell, perhaps you or even I will someday be a saint. With God's mercy, all things are possible! I surely will pray.

And thank you for the joy you wished me on our Lady's feast day. I shall hold that joy against my heart.

Under separate cover—also by airmail—I am sending you all the information that I possess about us.

I cannot truthfully say that "I left Friendship House." Does a mother ever leave her children, even if they leave her? Let us put it that way. That is one chapter in my life where darkness not only walked with me but swallowed me! Of this there is no need to speak.

Officially what happened was this. In 1951, at the Lay Apostolic Congress, I had a 2 hr. talk with Msgr. Montini, and a 15 minute talk with the

Pope. Both of them explained to me Secular Institutes. It seemed to be the desire of the Pope, and the advice of Msgr. Montini then Papal Secretary, that I not only pray over this idea but bring back the message I heard in Rome to everyone in FH. I did.

The one Canadian House, Madonna House, Combermere, known then as the Canadian Province of Friendship House, agreed to become a Secular Institute, dedicating their whole life to the apostolate, under the three vows of poverty, chastity and obedience.

U.S.A. Friendship House at the time, with six foundations, asked for time to think it over. They thought it over for five years. Then, at a special meeting, two houses decided to join us—Madonna House Secular Institute in the making—namely, Portland, Oregon and Washington, D.C. The rest decided to remain FREE CATHOLIC ACTION.

Through the enclosed literature you will see what our status is now. Incidentally, we are a Secular Institute in the making. We have five priests, plus laymen and laywomen. The official name for our Institute is Domus Dominae. The priests, who are a separate moral body under canon law, call themselves Domus Domini, but the public in general call us all Domus Dominae.

Eddie and I, incidentally, took vows of chastity four years ago. Eddie was his typical simple self—a very holy guy, that Irishman. He was so happy to see you recently. When asked if he wished to take this vow—otherwise I could not remain in Domus Dominae—his answer was, "Of course I wish to. So little to give for so much we have received."

At the present moment we have 5 foundations besides Madonna House, which is the Headquarters of Domus Dominae, or Madonna House: Marian Centre in Edmonton working with hoboes (we feed 400 a day); Maryhouse, Whitehorse, Y.T., working with transients, Indians, and the problems of a frontier town; Catholic Information Centre in Edmonton (self-evident); Casa de Nuestra Senora—the Mexican-Spanish-American apostolate, accent on children and youth; Stella Maris House, Portland, Oregon—a mandate on a broad interracial justice front (Mexican, Spanish-Americans, Negroes, Gypsies, Indians) and social justice work (Labour and Management and Housing). And Madonna House, Combermere, Training Centre for the apostolate; and a Rural Settlement House. All Houses mandated by respective Ordinaries.

The membership of the apostolate numbers about 60 at present; others expected. We have official invitations from Tanganyka, Uganda, Vietnam, Pakistan, West Indies, Chile.

Seems as if our Lady was giving us the world to restore to her son. Ora pro nobis.

Our present official status is that we are a pious union, fully approved by our ordinary, Bishop William Smith. Our constitutions (both priestly and lay) are at the present moment in Rome at the Congregation of Religious (Secular Institute Department) and are being processed. We have an advocate, a special priest, looking after the job. The hopes for approval this year are very high. Do pray that this might go through, please, as expected.

I guess that covers it, plus the literature that we will send to you air mail. This combination of letter and literature should clarify my present life and our Institute pretty well for you, dear Father Louis.

I have been tempted many times to write to you, and to tell you all that has transpired, of shadow and light. But something held me back. Instead, strange as this might seem, I prayed for you. While you were writing *The Sign of Jonas* I was going through my little Gethsemani with FH. There seemed to be no point in writing. We were very close. I have always marveled how close I have been to you, and to the Trappists of Kentucky, ever since you went there. Must be your prayers. For the silence of your place was as healing oil and wine to my many wounds, as I seem to lay on a thousand roads that were no roads at all, and yet were.

You need not ask me to pray for you. I pray for you and your intentions every day. I have never been near a Trappist monastery; and yet I seem to know yours pretty well. I do not know how or why, but it seems that I do.

I have never thought of you as a celebrity. I guess you are a big one at that; but to me, in a manner of speaking, you are a son. And in another sense, a Father. And in a third, a brother. And together we seek our Beloved.

Forgive me for writing to you about all this, but somehow it just comes out; and so I am putting it on paper.

Thank you for your prayers, and for the prayers of the good Novices. Both are powerful, and I need them so much in my utter poverty. For the older I get, the more clearly I see how utterly poor indeed I am.

May Lent bring you closer to Him whom you love so.

Lovingly and gratefully yours in our Lady, Catherine

# Catherine de Hueck Doherty to Thomas Merton

*August 26, 1958*

Dear Father Louie,

A thin parcel came in the mail the other day. It was late in the evening that I opened it, and found it was a meditation by you.

I have been reading it slowly at night, very slowly, enjoying every word, or should I say savoring it, for my heart is hungry for God.

I loved the beauty of the book, the paper, the printing. It made a good background for the beauty of thought.

Your inscription and autograph brought me joy. For a second or two a brilliant light shone, and I seemed to understand what is truly meant by the sentence, "in union of prayer in Christ our Lord." And my joy grew, and is still with me.

I am reading just now your latest book *Thoughts in Solitude.* It helps me so very much because, in a sense, I too have entered finally the solitude the Lord has prepared for me.

The word from Rome is that we are going to be approved soon, and our Institute erected, sometime, I hear, before Christmas, or right after it. The foundations of our Secular Institute of Laywomen—Domus Dominae, and an Institute of Laymen and clerics, Domus Domini. Together these two institutes will form the one apostolate of Madonna House. The women's Institute will be approved first, then the men's a few months later, so we are told.

At present I have moved to the office of Director General of the Women's Institute and the co-director of the apostolate with the Director General of the Men's Institute.

Both of us are occupying these positions "pro-tem" until the official election takes place after each Institute is erected. As far as I am concerned, I know that I will be elected by the majority of my spiritual female children. I don't *want to be* in the natural order, but it seems inevitable. So I am using this little short space of time left to me to enter God's Noviciate. For I have no other noviciate in order to meditate, to learn, to absorb one little sentence that must henceforth become my whole life: TO GOVERN IS TO LOVE. Pray that I may. Oh, pray that I may understand this and live it.

Strange, how clearly I see my utter poverty, how my nothingness un-rolls before me in its immensity. And yet, in its infinite smallness. I behold a strange sight—nothingness covered with all wounds of sin, with scabs of recent ones. Yet, I understand without understanding, that that poverty, that nothingness, will in some way, that seems a deep mystery, bring Christ to others, especially to those He has entrusted to me to lead to Him.

Because, if I'm open and simple, and not afraid or ashamed to show my poverty, my nothingness, my wounds and scabs, then per force all those who come in contact with me will be able to bypass my poor self, I hope, with pity and compassion and a prayer for me, and see Christ in His full-ness. For nothing will impede their sight. For nothingness cannot stand between another soul and its Creator, its Lover.

A strange coincidence happened. On our property we have a Russian Isba, built by a Russian architect many years ago. It used to be our priests' house; they lived there. But with the growth of the apostolate, they moved to other quarters. And St. Catherine of Siena, as we named the Isba, a log house, Russian style, was given over to me. And thus, I repeat, by a strange coincidence, I came to dwell at the evening of my life in a little bit of holy Russia. And Catherine the sinner finally came to rest in the arms of Cath-erine of Siena, the saint.

I feel at home in this lonely house on a little island amidst pine trees, separated from the mainland and the big house by a clumsy rustic bridge, built by our boys. It is a busy place during the daytime, but in the evening I have it to myself—my solitude. There is a fire place. It shares my solitude, and speaks to me of the Holy Ghost who is also fire, and Whom we in Rus-sia call "the Crimson Dove, the God of Love"!

You see why I need your prayers, Fr. Louie. There is so little time left for me to learn to love the Beloved, to begin to probe the saying TO GOV-ERN IS TO LOVE. Will you beseech Him in your solitude that I in mine may be a better pupil in my old age than I was in my youth.

Yes, in union of prayers in Christ our Lord, with deep gratitude and love, I remain, very affectionately yours, Catherine

## Thomas Merton to Catherine de Hueck Doherty

*September 18, 1958*

Dear Catherine,

Your deeply moving letter came the other day, just before I received from New York proofs of the *Secular Journal* . . . I wish you would look over the proofs of the preface and straighten out any errors. You are forbidden, under obedience, to delete any compliments addressed to your person . . .[13]

The great paradox of Superiorship is that no one can be a Superior unless he is fully worthy, and yet no one is fully worthy. There is only one solution: that Christ Himself, in us, must be the Superior, for He alone is worthy. And we must be content to struggle to keep out of His way. Above all, as you say so wisely, we must be glad if those under us *see* our defects, and are even aware of our sins in some way. Because that means that they will not expect too much from us, and will place their hopes in Christ. The crux of the whole "problem" of being a Superior is right there, in the shame we feel at letting everyone down, the shame at not being up to our task, the fear that everything will be known, that our nothingness will be seen and realized. So many Superiors, thrown into a panic by this fear, become harsh and demanding or suspicious and resentful. And that is not to "govern" but to "dominate." The same thing works the other way, of course, a hundred times over. Because there are subjects also who want to dominate, and who do not want the Superior to know their shame, and who try to get in the first blow . . . May God spare you from such.

In the end, though, the solution is Love—you have said it. And love, it seems to me, implies the realization that perhaps already those subject to us know our failings very well, and accept them with love, and would not dream of holding them against us, because they know these things do not matter. That is the great consolation: in the joy of being known and forgiven, we find it so much easier to forgive everything, even before it happens.

Pray for me, Catherine, in my own sins and struggles. After so boldly advertising to the world that I was out to become a saint, I find I am doing a pretty bum job of it. It is really funny, and I am not surprised or distressed to see what a damn fool I have been: maybe I have a

*Photograph of Catherine taken by Merton at a restaurant in 1941. Used with permission of Madonna House.*

*Merton with friends at St. Bonaventure on Commencement Day in 1941. Used with permission of The Thomas Merton Collection, Friedsan Library, St. Bonaventure University.*

*Friendship House in Harlem, where Merton volunteered for several weeks. Used with permission of Madonna House.*

*Catherine dictating letters in Harlem. Used with permission of Madonna House.*

*Merton's hermitage. Used with permission of the Merton Legacy Trust and the Thomas Merton Center at Bellarmine University.*

*Catherine at the entrance of the first poustinia at Madonna House. Used with permission of Madonna House.*

*Catherine at her poustinia in the winter. Used with permission of Madonna House.*

*Merton lecturing in Bangkok on the morning of December 10, 1968. Used with permission of the Merton Legacy Trust and the Thomas Merton Center at Bellarmine University*

call to that peculiarly Russian form of sanctity—*yurodivetsvo*—to be a fool for Christ and to really enjoy it, in a quiet and inconspicuous way, because in a way He enjoys it . . .

But it certainly is a wonderful thing to wake up suddenly in the solitude of the woods and look up at the sky and see the utter nonsense of *everything,* including all the solemn stuff given out by professional asses about the spiritual life: and simply to burst out laughing, and laugh and laugh, with the sky and the trees because God is not in words, and not in systems, and not in liturgical movements, and not in "contemplation" with a big C, or in asceticism or in anything like that, not even in the apostolate. Certainly not in books. I can go on writing them, for all that, but one might as well make paper airplanes out of the whole lot.

I must stop now and devote myself to the folly of getting up a conference for the novices. But it is not so bad: I prepare conferences and then tell them something entirely different. If I gave them what I had prepared, then that would really be folly.

Catherine, one of my mad ideas—which is really mad and I don't pay attention to it—is to break off and start a new kind of small monastery in Ecuador, a sort of an ashram for local intellectuals and men of good will and Indians, part of the time devoted to discussions and spiritual works of mercy (and some corporal, like a clinic) and part of the time devoted to sitting in a hermitage and getting the straws out of my hair. The whole thing from a certain aspect looks more like Madonna House than O.C.S.O. [Order of Cistercians of the Strict Observance]. Anyway, there is no indication that it would possibly be the will of God, or at least not in the extreme form, and so I put it away as a temptation . . .

affectionately in Christ Our Lord, fr. m. Louis

*Catherine de Hueck Doherty to Thomas Merton*

*September 25, 1958*

Dear Father Louie,

You sure put some obedience on me—and I mean it! This is the second time you have done this to me—but the first time unexpectedly, in *Seven Storey Mountain*. But this time openly, and with an obedience not to change anything.

That was my first reaction. And my second was to laugh, and say to myself, "Katia, indeed, you are a fool. Be simple about those things. If this good priest wants to tell people what he is telling them, then rejoice, and offer it all to the Lord with gratitude. For after all is said and done, you are 58 years old, and you've been in the apostolate for 29 years. And outside of Father Merton nobody had anything too good to say about you. So, if he does, accept it as the oil and wine of a good Samaritan. Yes, be simple about it."

And so I was. And I thank you, and the Lord, for the oil and the wine.

There was very little correction to do; and what there was, we did. Straightening out the matter of the Pope, we expect the approval from the Sacred Congregation of Religious, as I wrote, before Christmas, or soon afterwards. And I escaped from *Russia* and not from Finland, but through Finland. Outside of that, there were no corrections.

Your good letter certainly cheered me up.

I don't think Ecuador is the place to start an ashram. Personally I am all for India. That is where they would really go over big, and bring to the Church a lot of people. Who knows whether it is a mad idea or not. Trappists have been known to do madder things than that. And maybe even a clinic would be possible, on account of the Pope really has radical ideas about contemplatives, or so I hear. I would consider it a higher vocation, in a manner of speaking. Maybe the Pope would too. He is terrific, and has the vision of the whole that leaves us all behind as back numbers.

Speaking of vocations now. Believe it or not, I have a Trappist problem on my hands. And what I mention to you now is DEFINITELY IN CONSCIENCE, bound with the seal of the confessional, and double-bound, for it concerns one of your monks. He has been sending us young people—

one, in fact—and is planning to send us another who is leaving, I think, at the expiration of his vows; and he is sending other friends to see us.

And, of course, all this is very welcome. I like giving hospitality to the friends of the Trappists. But, he wants to join us, the Domus Domini part of our apostolate (the Institute for laymen and clerics). It forms part of our Secular Institute, the other being an Institute for women (Domus Dominae).

He definitely makes me feel terribly unhappy. I don't know why. There are many Trappists I know, or at least I have heard about, who leave their Order. In fact, there is one in Canada here who secularized himself and is very happy; and that is okay by me.

Frankly, I wouldn't be shocked at all if you went and started your Ashram. For there is in you something I understand as a Russian, I think. I myself call it the "search of the Absolute," or the "search for the Absolute," the holy restlessness of God.

I find myself bereft of words to tell the difference between inner feelings that I have regarding your re-occurring waves towards that strange goal, and the shrinking, the strange fear, the desire to arise and lift my hands to heaven, and stand between [the Trappist in question here]. "Someone" seems to attract him. I have a desire to protect—and forgive me this horrible simile—to shake Father till his teeth rattle and he gets some sense into his head. And, yet, there is a strange cringing in me at the same time. It is so darn unusual (I almost said "damn"). I am afraid of having overstepped limits of some sort in advising a priest.

I am enclosing a copy of my letter to him for your perusal, under the seal of the confessional again. Please return it to me. I don't feel I can send you his letter of many pages, for it probably is confidential in some sort of a way; but the very fact that he has written so much and says so little, bothers me.

And the reasons he adduces are somehow all wrong, or seem to me to be; but I must confess, I am confused.

You see Tom—I mean Father Louie—I love the Trappists with a great love. I love them all. What I say about them is true. And it hurts somehow, beyond a human hurt, as if Christ was sad, or something like that. Well, that is cockeyed, isn't it? But there it is. And somehow, for some unknown reason, I am walking in the unknown in all this deal, or so it seems. And I probably make no sense at all to you either, even less than to myself. But, I repeat, somehow I want to turn to you and tell you about it, because you are in the same place; because you can do something, maybe. Perhaps you can pray in some special way for him. I don't know what, but I am worried.

Yah, writing those books must be quite something. A sort of crucible. The silent Monk that talks on paper. Console yourself though: your silence speaks very well, especially between the lines. I'm still slowly reading *Thoughts in Solitude*. And once in a while I pick up some of your other books and get renewed courage to go on. Yes, your silence speaks well between the lines; and your words mean more than they seem to mean.

As for praying for you Fr. Louie, I do that, ever more often as time goes by. Somehow you come closer with its passing.

Thanks for the words of wisdom on superiorship. THAT REALLY HELPED ME. And I was so happy that you understood why I am so glad that those under me see my defects. I have tried to tell that to a few priests, but somehow it all fell flat. Yes, you are right: Christ must be in the superior, or otherwise everything would go to pot everywhere.

And caritas is the answer. Thanks.

I hope I haven't burdened you too much with my Trappist problem.

Affectionately in Mary, Catherine

# III. Letters: 1960–68

## Thomas Merton to Catherine de Hueck Doherty

*The following is a note of Merton's appended to a letter to Catherine by Brother Gabriel, one of Merton's novices.*

*February 24, 1961*

Hello Catherine!

I was glad to hear a little about Madonna House from this good priest who is visiting here. I think he seems to have a very good vocation—keep him and myself in your prayers. And blessing on you and Madonna House.

In Our Lady, Fr. M. Louis

*Catherine de Hueck Doherty to Thomas Merton*

*March 17, 1961*

Dearly beloved Father Louis,

I haven't thanked you yet for the beautiful inscription on the wonderful book *God Is My Life*. I received it on December 8, the same day as I was given the Papal medal, *Pro Ecclesia et Pontifice*.

I received the latter reverently and gratefully, but with complete bewilderment and astonishment. I received your book joyfully. And it is still on my table, and I still look at it; and what is more, it looks at me, silently, and teaches me the things I want to know so passionately, so constantly. Some pages teach me more than others, but all bring me peace.

There is much in my heart that I would like to share with you but then it comes to me that you know it already. One thing I want to tell you about is that I have returned to the ways of my people. When confronted with the tragic sight of man ignoring God (I would prefer if he rebelled against Him), I decided to go back to the "poustinia" of my people. In my childhood, my father used to tell me when I meet evil in a new form "that such are dealt with through fasting and prayer—the two arms that man can lift to God always—and go into the desert." (He never used the word "retiring"—but always going forward, as it were. "Desert" in Russian means "Poustinya.")

So now, every Friday, I go into the silence of the Lord. It is at times like these that I have many interesting conversations with you and with other brothers of mine in the Trappist Monastery. Strange is it not—or is it? How simply one can meet in the silence of the love of God.

Thank you for the book. Thank you for allowing Fr. Gabriel to write. He went through so much pain—this good and holy priest—and now he has found a place where pain becomes joy, if he lets it.

Lovingly yours in Mary, Catherine

*Catherine de Hueck Doherty to Thomas Merton*

*May 26, 1961*

Dear Father Louis,

Lately I have been in great agony of spirits and so I come knocking at your door, asking for the alms of your prayers—not to remove the agony of spirits. For I realize that it is an immense grace to a poor soul like me to be able to share a little in Christ's agony in Gethsemani. I beg of the Lord the gift of faith and fortitude to stand still, as I so greatly desire to do.

Strange as it might seem, my agony of spirit is connected with the world as a whole. It appears to me as if the human Church was asleep and Christ is vainly trying to wake it up. Or to put it another way, the masses of the laity have clothed their souls in asbestos suits so that the fire of the Holy Ghost may not impenetrate us nor set us on fire.

Frankly, I have no words to express what is happening to me, but I don't think I need to. You will know without words. Just give me the alms of your prayers.

I enclose a poem of no poetical importance, I imagine, but it too tries to tell what is in my soul.

Lovingly yours in Mary, Catherine

*Thomas Merton to Catherine de Hueck Doherty*

*July 22, 1961*

Dear Catherine,

Your letter was written on May 26 (anniversary of my ordination) and here we are already at the Feast of St. Mary Magdalen. I am sorry for all the delay, but I did want to acknowledge your letter with at least a brief note of some sort. Your two poems were very welcome and they will be posted on the novices' board for their enlightenment. They can use some. I keep trying to remind them that they are not alone in the world, and that they have brethren suffering and struggling very often with much greater problems than we have here, and much greater difficulties. We remain pretty bound up in our relatively small concerns.

However, no one is exempt from anguish. I share the agony of spirits you speak of, and for the same reasons. There is no doubt that we are all involved in a social structure that is rotting from within. The fact that so many good people are able to identify this futile and transient structure with Christian civilization or even, worse still, the body of Christ, is enough to cause anyone agony. I think this agony is simply the inevitable form our suffering takes at such a time. We feel useless, bound, helpless . . . We are stopped, blocked, tongue-tied. When we open our mouths we run into so much contradiction that we wonder whether or not we can believe our own convictions. As Christians we are not really "with" any of the big social movements in one direction or another, left or right. We no longer have the support of a really Christian society. When we lean on the society that is built on what used to be Christian, it gives way and we fall with it . . . yet we cannot commit ourselves to the even more transient secularism that claims to possess the key to the future. It is a very salutary solitude, and one in which I for one think more and more that I will have to stop preaching or to preach only by silence, because no matter what you say, you seem to be saying yes to something you cannot in conscience approve of.

I send you a poem in return for yours. Not exactly a nice little spiritual nosegay. Pray that I may be allowed to print it somewhere. That is not yet by any means certain. I will send along one on the "bomb" which, by some miracle, is getting printed ["Original Child Bomb"] . . .[14]

Very Cordially in Christ Our Lord, fr. m. Louis

## Catherine de Hueck Doherty to Thomas Merton

Pax Caritas

*March 17, 1962*

Dear Father Louie,

Are you weary? With the terrible weariness of one who stands before our "man-made hell"; before the surrealistic desert in which modern man lives in company of dead, twisted trees of his sick imagination? Drinking in the stagnant waters, polluted by himself? The only escape he seems to know are tranquillizers, and endless sessions (if he can afford them) with psychiatrists, with whom he can talk endlessly on the subject that makes up his world and his god—HIMSELF!

For some reason I think you are weary. I know I am frightened and weary too. For the face of the Prince of Darkness is becoming clearer and clearer to me. It seems he does not care any more to remain "the great anonymous one," the "incognito," the "everyone." He seems to have come into his own and shows himself in all his tragic reality. So few believe in his existence that he does not need to hide himself anymore!

One can "see him" if one knows him, almost as he is. The sight is frightening. It seems to me that especially Russian souls recognize him more easily because they have always warned and taught about him. That is why they turn to the Bogoroditza [She who gave birth to God] and ask her to protect us from his wiles. Those who do not know him do not know her either . . . THE ONE HE FEARS.

You write about our responsibility, about war and peace. You cry out in agony, that we each have a voice that must be raised! Keep crying. We need your tired yet strong voice. But know too that you are truly crying in a wilderness, a wilderness full of dead-ends, where no voice penetrates.

It is into those dead-ends that we, lay apostles, must carry God's message, must bring His voice with which you blend yours so well. For, of course, you realize, Fr. Louie, that the Harlems of the USA which you and I knew so well are today a paradise compared to any place in the world, be it a private house amidst gardens and lawns, an apartment house in a huge city or a small town, the midst of the marts of trade, the suburbs, or the wide open spaces of foreign mission lands or home ones. All of these separately, and all of them put together, are more tragic, more hellish, than our "Harlems" ever were.

Take us, for instance, here at Madonna House and its ten foundations or missions. In Combermere we have yearly two Summer Schools of the Lay Apostolate, one for single laymen and women (all of them young), the other for married couples. Some four hundred people pass through Madonna House's Blue Door, painted blue in honor of Our Lady. And through the balance of the year, according to our latest count, close to 2,000 people come to MH to visit through the year to stay a while—some for a week, some for several weeks, others for a month or two, and others for a week-end.

What is so tragic, so frightening, so shattering to me is that most of them are sick, profoundly sick, sick of soul, sick of mind and of heart. Yet each is hungry for the Absolute—for God. Yet, each is frightened of meeting Him, because, as they tell me, poor souls, they are all frightened of pain. And He is a Crucified God. They are also afraid of making decisions, of taking responsibility. No wonder, for how can they make decisions when emotionally they are "children," children in the bodies of men and women. Some of them have already begotten their own children.

In them the image of God seems disintegrated already. Yet we, the Lay Apostles of the Lord, must restore it. Coute que coute! [No matter what the cost.] Yes, we must restore that image, even, if necessary, at the price of our own lives.

Neuroses? Yes, of course. Our century suffers from it. We all know that. But to me at times, who has to deal so very much with it (I doubt if you knew that I am a nurse and have had some postgraduate work in psychiatry, which I kept fairly hidden in Harlem). It is a strange neurosis that appears at times to be "manipulated by Satan" for his own ends. It seems to me at times again that I am dealing with puppets who are hanging or dangling on strings that he keeps in his hands. It is at moments like this that my soul cries out in the darkest of nights, BECAUSE GOD—neurosis or no neurosis—IS IGNORED BY PEOPLE WHO STILL HAVE A WILL THAT CAN FUNCTION, A REASON STILL ILLUMINAT-ED BY FAITH THAT KNOWS QUITE WELL THE DIFFERENCE BETWEEN GOOD AND EVIL BUT DOESN'T DO ANYTHING ABOUT IT.

Oh! if they were only cold or hot, BUT THEY ARE TEPID, SO TEPID THAT EVEN I FEEL LIKE VOMITING THEM OUT OF MY MOUTH! BUT HOW CAN I, when my soul loves them with a passionate love. My Beloved died for them and they are His!

Yet, we lay apostles MUST GO into those dead-ends where the voice of God is not heard. We must enter the revolting tepidity of modern souls. We must have the courage to face Satan in his own domain!

True, modern lay apostolic groups are working hard at many angles. But, Father Louie, I confess that fear grips me again. For I have attended, just last year, so many conventions, conferences, executive meetings and non-executive meetings of the lay apostolate, that it even tires me to remember their numbers.

As a result of all those contacts, I have developed almost a problem of conscience. At times I think I am literally going crazy under the stress and strain of such meetings. I fear with a great fear that I may be proud, proud enough to allow myself to sit in judgment on my betters. Then I tremble before the Lord lest this be true, and search my heart endlessly. I do not really find, as far as I can see, any of those fearsome symptoms, but instead I find sadness, and a tremendous compassionate love, filled with but one desire: to shout to my fellow lay apostles at those conferences, conventions, THAT NOTHING MATTERS EXCEPT *CARITAS!*

For the lay groups, with a few exceptions these days, seem to set such a tremendous value on college degrees, on technical skills, on "worldly competence." Oh, I know, all this must be taken into consideration. Love uses all tools, and uses them well. But nevertheless, CARITAS in my estimation should come first.

I'm sure that I do not express myself clearly, for words kind of tumble out of my heart, tripping over one another. I remember when I began in Harlem in 1938, Fr. LaFarge asked me, "What techniques" I planned to use in Harlem?[15] I remember being confused by his question. For I never connected "love" with any technique in particular.

To me, it all began, continued, and ended with CARITAS. All I wanted to do is go to live with my brother, the Negro, in grave humility, with a heart filled with gratitude, that under the existing circumstances, he, the Negro, would even allow me to live with him.

Living and serving his needs, as the Lord revealed them to me day by day, hour by hour, was all the technique that I knew. That is how even now I have trained my spiritual children to go forth to their missions, like the West Indies, for instance. (Incidentally I am enclosing the mandate of the Ordinary of that diocese for your perusal. It is the type of mandate that my heart understands.)

At one Latin American lay apostolic conference recently I truly couldn't stand it any more. There was a discussion on the rostrum about worldly competency, about degrees and skills. Throughout the long day I never once heard the word *caritas* mentioned. Perhaps it was presumed. But as the conference went on, the Latin American contingent that came to observe, became very angry and restless because of this stress on worldly competence. By implication, it bespoke of some sort of superiority on the American part of the participants. And it appeared to me that the bonds of charity were broken right then and there somehow. How, I couldn't clearly define.

So, unable to contain my heart any longer, I got up and spoke, almost with violence, and yet with tears flowing down my face—silly old woman that I am. I spoke about the need for caritas, primarily, about the need for grave humility, and about being a servant more than a teacher.

The Latin Americans somehow understood me and responded; but our own were very, very angry with this. Was I right to raise my voice? Was it the right place to raise it? Was it the right time?

So it seems to me that before we can talk about war and peace, before you or I or anyone can expect the voices of men to be raised for peace against armaments, we somehow must bring men face to face with God. He alone is the reason for our standing up and being counted, for taking responsibilities for our actions, even if those responsibilities and the taking of them will lead us into prison and death.

How to do this? Especially, how should we Lay Apostles, who must and can go where no one else wants to or can penetrate—into the jungles of modern souls, into the obscene man-made deserts and sterile hells—how are we to do this?

First, I feel, by stripping ourselves. For only the Lay Apostles who are "nakedly following the naked Christ," and who are fully cognizant of their utter poverty, can do this in Him WITHOUT WHOM WE CAN DO NOTHING.

We must, it seems to me, be the "dispossessed ones," the "detached ones." For only then can we be truly attached to God.

The way to that detachment, that dis-possession, is contemplation. Perhaps I think of it as "contemplation a la Russe." Would it work in America? I don't know, for I know so little "je begaye comme un enfant [I stammer like a baby]." And yet, why is it that I so strongly feel that I am on the right path?

You wrote the Preface for the book ALONE WITH GOD. I believe strangely enough, crazily enough, that a lay apostle can be, and should be, a hermit in the world. For there are inner deserts and cells to go to, where a soul learns that poverty, that detachment from itself, that is needed to enter the fight between Darkness and Light, the fight not only for oneself, but for all those we must reach in all those fearsome places. I believe that we can pray always. And that our constant prayer these days, especially, must be very forceful, a sort of begging God, like the man in the Gospel, who kept knocking, asking for bread. I repeat—it must be FOR GROWTH IN FAITH!

I feel that God will not refuse this prayer for FAITH. For He knows what we must face. And knows that FAITH, that COURAGE that will lead us into the modern NO-MAN'S LAND. For where are the books anyhow that can tell us about it? For never has such a NO-MAN'S LAND been known before. So the Lord must grant us this FAITH, this KNOWLEDGE, that will increase our caritas, that will enable us to enter it.

Father Louie, you know all about these things. You too have been and are walking these inner deserts as well as the outward ones. Giving men who abide there living bread and living waters to eat and drink. You are familiar with all their paths, with all these dark and fearsome places. So you know too what we Lay Apostles of the Lord must be, and what we must do, to arise and go there, as go we must!

Will you write about that? Write for our little paper RESTORATION.[16] Write for Lay Apostles, the "pebbles of the Lord," the ones he bade David to use against Goliath. I think we, God's pebbles, Lay Apostles, have been long enough in the "brook of God's graces," and hence are polished enough to fit into His hand. But we must be more. Tell us how we are to be more polished.

We are so small, the band of MH proper: only 104, counting everyone— priests, laymen, laywomen. But our paper goes far, even though it is small, or perhaps because of that. Don't be afraid to speak simply, because we are simple, and in the eyes of the world not too important. We shall, I know, understand your simplicity, your loving, profound simplicity. For God permits that such simplicity be revealed to His little ones, and we are His littlest.

Tell us of poverty. We are poor in so many ways and we have learned to love our poverty. But in us burns a hunger to walk deeper into her domain. Show us the way therein. Tell us about our need for the TOTALITY of our stripping. Tell us how needful is contemplation in its TOTALITY too, especially for us who must be contemplatives, and in a way, hermits in the busy market place.

Tell us of the constant prayer of the heart, which in the west you call the prayer of the presence of God, the prayer my people loved so, so that we may learn to apply it to our strange, frightening modern world. Tell us of LOVE, LOVE that joyously desires to identify itself with the poor who live in palaces as well as in the slums, and in all the places in between. For today so many are poor everywhere, in so many thousands of different and frightening ways.

I know I am asking much. But, Father, fearsome is the night, close is the Evil One, dark the way. Feed us the words of life, for He had chosen us to go, seemingly, where no one else wants to go, or perhaps can go.

I pray much for you. Don't laugh at me when I say that oftener and oftener it seems I come to Gethsemani, and even pray at your side there. For the Lord gives me the grace of vigils these days. For it is hard to sleep when one is searching, searching for ways and means to extend His kingdom deeper into the soul of man.

For the Lord is close to Madonna House in the strangest ways. For instance, recently the non-discalced Carmelites have been here. Of all things they wish to establish a hermitage near us!

It develops that there is a growing demand amongst them, especially the younger element, for the contemplative life!! Up to now, that Carmelite Order had a spot in Austria—the mountains of the Tyrol—to which a few chosen priests were sent from time to time to spend a year in solitude and prayer. But now that the demand is growing, the top superiors sent a Carmelite to Combermere to look the place over, for we are located in the Laurentian Mountains with much wilderness still left around about us; and also they seem for an unknown reason, at least unknown to me, to wish to be not too far from MH. Anyhow, they really made a thorough survey, and already half of their Council or more are in favor of it.

But Our Lady of Combermere has not stopped there. And what I am telling you in this paragraph, dear Father Louis, IS TOLD UNDER THE SEAL—STRICTLY CONFIDENTIAL: one of your own men (but not from your House) has received permission to be a Hermit. He too asked if he could be one here near Madonna House. This is quite feasible, incidentally, as we have about 1,000 acres of wild hills and mountains, with rivers and lakes and forests. The permission has been granted. He will be coming soon.

Truly strange is my life. In Russia the Hermetical, as well as the Cenobitical, life always went together in the old days, and I understand still do. And here I am, a lonely Russian, far away from all these ways of the Lord, in exile, whose end will not necessarily end in glory, whom the Lord consoles by bringing both ways close to me.

You must be tired of writing books. Here Holy Obedience must be a tremendous strength for you. I wish you could be that Hermit [here at Madonna House]. But then, I guess that would be wrong, unless God wished it.

Please, let us pray for each other. But, especially, you pray for me. At times, God forgive me, I think we are both miscast somehow into the wrong century. This is rank heresy, of course, so FIAT LORD, NOT WHAT I WILL BUT WHAT YOU WILL. And I know you, Fr. Louie, do too, say FIAT. Yet, why is it that I want to say to you—COURAGE, as if you needed it! Forgive me.

Lovingly in the Incomprehensible Beloved Lord, Catherine

P.S. The hermit in question that I wrote to you about under the Seal wants me to ask you URGENTLY where I could get hold of for him the CONSUETUDINES OF BLESSED RUDOLF, a Camaldolese hermit and general of his Order back in 1080. Could you drop me a tiny little note in answer to that request?

## Thomas Merton to Catherine de Hueck Doherty
[*Cold War Letter 79*][17]

*June 4, 1962*

Dear Catherine,

Your long, wonderful letter has gone for nearly three months without an answer. But you can guess all the reasons. And now perhaps if I answer it is because the voice which was shouting, momentarily, about peace, has been told to shut up. And I have a little time to return to other things such as writing letters.

I knew I didn't have much time to get said what I felt ought to be said. So I got it all out as best I could, in a jumble of words and articles, and even finished a book. The book is on stencils, and when the last stencil was typed the order came in not to print or publish anything more on topics "not befitting a contemplative monk." Apparently the most crucial problems, and the struggle with the demon, these are out of range of a contemplative monk. I was told it would be all right if I prayed over these matters, however.

You ask me if I am weary? Sure. Perhaps not as weary as you are, but weary in the same way, weary of the same things. It is complicated by the fact that one is tempted to feel he has no right to be weary of the actions and pronouncements of a lot of very good, sincere people who are themselves weary of something or other. We are like a bunch of drunken men at the last end of a long stupid party falling over the furniture in the twilight of dawn. I hope it is dawn. Probably not, though. But the thing that eats one up is the anguish over the Church. This of course leaves me inarticulate because I know that anyone can show where and how and why I am not a good Catholic, a good Christian, a faithful member of Christ. And yet there is this conviction that the Church is full of a terrible spiritual sickness, even though there is always that inexpressible life . . .

It is at such a time as this that one has to have faith in the Church, and the fact that we suffer from the things that make us suffer, the fact that we cannot find any way out of the suffering, is perhaps a sign of hope. I do not pretend to understand the situation or to analyze anything. Your answer is correct. What is wanted is love. But love has been buried under words, noise, plans, projects, systems, and apostolic gimmicks. And when we open our mouths to do something about it we add more words, noise, plans, etc. We are afflicted with the disease of constant talking with almost nothing to say. From that point of view I suppose it is just as well that I am saying nothing more about the war business. Saying things does not help. Yet what is there to do? You're right again, that what one must do is meet the needs that He brings before us, when and as He does so. We will not see anything clear, but we must do His will. We have to be heroic in our obedience to God. And that may mean cutting through a whole forest of empty talk and clichés and nonsense just to begin to find some glimmer of His will. To obey always and not know for sure if we are really obeying. That is not fun at all, and people like to get around the responsibility by entering into a routine of trivialities in which everything seems clear and noble and defined: but when you look at it honestly it falls apart, for it is riddled with absurdity from top to bottom . . .

With all friendship in Christ, Tom

*Catherine de Hueck Doherty to Thomas Merton*

*October 11, 1962*

Dear Father Louis,

Your letter of June 4 has remained unanswered for a long time. But I know that you did not expect an immediate answer. For that is the way it has always been between us.

Your letter came to me like a cry in the night, a very dark cry, a desperate cry, in a way, out of a very dark night. Strangely enough, it found a profound echo in my soul.

For I have been wrestling with powers and principalities, and my soul has been in an agonizing travail. Especially your articles on peace and against nuclear warfare bit deeply; but even before I read your articles in so many magazines, I was already in a strange agony.

You might have noticed that publicly I haven't written very much. I don't know if you have seen RESTORATION, but I am cutting out the two articles I have written as a result of your letter of June 4. I call them "Quo Vadis." They will tell you—for you know how to read behind the lines—the agony that I speak of to you, which was and is much more profound than I can express in any words. But I know it doesn't come anywhere near your agony.

Strange to say, I too, in the dark of the night—and I mean the physical night that comes to us when the day is done—have cried out to God for an increase of faith, a torrent of it. For if there is anything that we need now, it is faith.

I felt the pain, the urgency, that must have been in your soul. Though you have said much, you didn't say all that was to be said, and obedience closed your mouth. And the book lies gathering dust that might have made such a difference to the world.

If I could laugh at the same time as I cry, I would laugh, only it would be a sort of tragic, clownish laugh. But a contemplative monk is allowed at least to pray over the matters that tear the world apart.

We are both weary, weary with the same weariness. We are both in pain, at least a good kind of pain, because it is the pain of Christ. This pain of Christ eats me up, walks with me night and day, and will not let me be one second. Yet, it seems I am alone in my world with a few exceptions. For people are blind to the pain of Christ.

There is some kind of slow crucifixion in the thought that CHRIST IS NOT LOVED IN THIS WORLD. And when you want to raise your voice to make Him loved, you are told to shut up, you don't know what you are talking about.

As yet, I see no dawn, nothing but the night. God will strip some souls and again use His spittle and clay to open their eyes, and His finger to open their ears. I don't know, but I am crying because I cannot give up, and neither can you.

Few of us understand, Father Louis, how sick the Church is. Yet, as you say, it is the Mystical Body of Christ, the Bride of God, and Hell will not prevail against it. But I see catacombs, and I welcome them. For the only thing that will purify the Church from its sickness, I think, is martyrdom of the West. Something has to happen. I think what has to happen is that the blood of the martyrs again, once more, must wash human souls clean.

I fear for the Apostolate, even the lay apostolates that were so full of youth and zeal and newness, and simplicity. They are in danger of growing old in the midst of their youth. Organizational man is putting his cold fingers on the Apostolate. The Lay Apostolate has become a controversial, important No. 1 subject. Thousands of words are used up to describe it in our papers. It is spoken of on radio and it appears on TV. But simplicity is dying, and so is charity.

All things get organized, and canon lawyers move in. I was in Rome and spoke to the Sacred Congregation of Religious. They were quizzing me about our Apostolate. One Prelate asked, "How do you raise your finances?" Simply, I answered, "by begging." "What is your overhead?" said another. Simply, I answered, "Two cents on the dollar. The rest goes to the poor." "Do you believe that the Gospel can be lived in the 20th century?" asked the first Prelate. "Impossible," said the second, "I never heard of two cents on the dollar."

So, I proceeded to prove that for 32 years—I am celebrating my 32nd anniversary this Monday, on the feast of St. Theresa of Avila, the great contemplative—that is how we existed, and that is how I propose to exist, believing with my whole mind, my whole heart and soul, that the Gospel in its pristine purity can be lived and must be lived. It is the only answer to our disintegrating world.

And then I talked about poverty that lives on two cents of a dollar overhead. Do you know what I got as an answer—sub sigillo [in confidence] to you? I got a lecture on prudence. I heard them before, but this was really something.

Do you wonder that I went to St. Peter's and knelt before the Pieta of Michelangelo and wept and cried out to the Lord for the gift of Faith. Some janitor found me there hours later and told me that they are closing St. Peter's now, and that I had better go.

*You* are told to shut up, and *I* am told to be prudent about the Gospel and about poverty. Are there any comments necessary? Except the repetition of my favorite psalm, "Out of the depth I cry out to Thee, O Lord."

Why do I write all these things to you, dear Father Louis, who has enough of a cross to carry of his own? Well, the only answer is that there is no one else I could write to, and that writing to you once in a while is like meeting a Samaritan who puts oil and wine on my wounds JUST BY EXISTING, JUST BY BEING ACCESSIBLE through a postage stamp.

Yet, at the same time, I want to be that Samaritan to you, too. All I can offer you is the wine and oil of my love, the oil of my understanding, the inn of my heart, and the alms of my prayers, humble as they may be. Sometimes it helps to know that someone loves, shares and understands your pain. That's all I have to offer, these few little gifts.

A team of ours is leaving for East Pakistan. Will you remember them in your prayers? It is our 10th mission that goes forth to serve in simplicity and charity, poverty and grave humility, to serve in very humble ways our brothers in Christ, far across the seas. All I hope from that team, all I pray for, is that they may show those who do not believe that the Gospel can live in the 20th century, it really can.

Under holy obedience of my spiritual director I have collected the poems that I have written through the years. I send them to you, not because they are good poems; I have no illusions about that. But because you might find in one or the other an echo of your pain, and maybe it will console you again, and give you new strength. We need you so much, Father Louis, we who bear the heat of the market place.

In Mary, lovingly, Catherine

## Thomas Merton to Catherine de Hueck Doherty

*November 12, 1962*

Dear Catherine,

I was deeply moved by the Poustinia [i.e., hermitage] project. That is ideal. It is just right. It will be a wonderful contribution. It is the kind of thing that is most needed. And though it is certain that we must speak if and when we can, silence is always more important. The crises of the age are so enormous and the mystery of evil so unfathomable: the action of well-meaning men is so absurd and tends so much to contribute to the very evils it tries to overcome: all these things should show us that the real way is prayer, and penance, and closeness to God in poverty and solitude. Yet there is no question that sometimes this too is also preached as an invasion of responsibility. It is a terrible situation, and each case must be judged on its merits, with fear and trembling, by the gift of Counsel. Indeed it is very hard now to simply lay down a line of action and say this is it. I will not deviate from this. The next moment you may be forced to change your direction.

So it is usually when I have just resolved firmly to be perfectly silent that I find I have to speak: and when I have resolved to speak out boldly, that I am reduced to silence. At the moment I am pretty well reduced to silence on the war question, and that is all right. It is what I expected, and what I accept. And yet behind it is an evasion, a failure to measure up to the test of the times, for the Church has been too slow to speak and to take a definite position, and this has been weakness and betrayal on the part of those whose responsibility it was: they have been too deeply identified with secular interests.

. . . On the other hand I have the greatest sympathy for the rough and tumble peace movement with its all kinds of wacky people. They are certainly not saints, and some of them think themselves atheists. They are not all leading what we would call good lives. Yet perhaps the peace movement, begun imperfectly and followed with all kinds of errors and misjudgments, may be their way to find the real meaning of love. I know many such people who have despaired of finding love in our cold institutional gatherings and our official pronouncements. God alone knows what He means to do through these people. And He knows too that they are not easy to handle or to live with, for Dorothy

Day has had her share of difficulty with them. And yet they are there, and I suppose it is my job to be at least remotely the Church's arm around them, as nobody else much (in the clergy) seems interested.

. . . I think what I need to learn is an almost infinite tolerance and compassion. At least this is I think my great need, because negative thought gets nowhere. I am beginning to think that in our time we will correct almost nothing, and get almost nowhere: but if we can just prepare a compassionate and receptive soil for the future, we will have done a great work. I feel at least that this is the turn my own life ought to take.

. . . This must end here, though there would be much more to say. I am editing and correcting a manuscript of a Russian Orthodox scholar called Bolshakoff, who is at Oxford but doesn't write very good English. It is about the Russian mystics and full of very interesting material . . .

Yours in Christ, Tom Merton

## Catherine de Hueck Doherty to Thomas Merton

Pax Caritas

*May 8, 1963*

Dear Father Louis,

There are between our letters long periods of silence. I know you do not mind this, in fact I know and understand why it should be so, at least it seems to me you do.

You know, of course, that I love you much in the Lord. For it was He Who brought us together in FH for such a short spell of time. And yet, out of that meeting much has happened to me. In a strange manner I feel like an older sister or even mother to you. Why? I cannot tell. Maybe it isn't even that at all—yet there is a bond.

I know little about your life, except from your books, and the stray pieces of information that come my way. Yet, it seems I know much about you in another way, for I suffer with you. There are times when I suffer intensely too, when a deep darkness comes over me for you, or, as if I had to enter your darkness. We have a Russian word that means interiorizing the suffering of another, to share pain with that other, to be Simon to his passion, Veronica to his pain. To a Russian this is a natural and simple outcome of oneness, of the concept of the Mystical Body of Christ. Sharing, atoning, weeping with and for all the world, or a special person in it. It is loving. I mean all the above in the sense of the bond that I feel strongly is between us, especially in me toward you. I know not about you, but I think it is the same.

Now such a bond requires speech (letters) rarely. Yet it does require such speech in God's time. So I leave your letter to His time. In the meantime I pray over your last letter, and for you intensely. Now "God's time has come."

I am sitting in our Poustinia—desert—in an old simple farm house, in a plain whitewashed room that has only an eight-foot crucifix painted black, with a Fr. Charles de Foucauld sign on it. A wood stove is burning. It is still cold here as the house is high on a mountain top. The nearest neighbors are a mile away. There is nary a living soul around. All is solitude and silence. Rolling meadows and mountain ridges on the horizon, broken by forest lines, are all one can see.

It is a Russian landscape, and I find myself at long last *at home,* because I am where I belong. I feel free, and want to write to you whose spirit is so close to the spirit of the Eastern Churches and spirituality.

Fr. Louis, you have realized, of course, that God has raised you as a "sign of contradiction to many." You have understood that you must be THE HUNGRY ONE WHO WILL NOT BE FILLED IN THIS LIFE. For your hunger will spill over (hungry men must cry their hunger) and feed many. You know, of course, that you too have been "lifted up," crucified on the Crucifix of noise, people, places. You, the seeker of silence and solitude, in reality live in a show-window with thousands of eyes looking you over, thousands of hands stretched out to you, thousands of feet marching towards you, thousands of minds set on one thing—to see and to hear and to touch you, in a manner of speaking.

But there is more: you are and know you are part of this world and [part of] the Church. God has chosen you to suffer for it and for Her, with it and with Her. I heard Fr. Berrigan's tapes about you, and I wept silently for you, wishing foolishly perhaps that your rule forbade such tapings.

Like Christ—because of Christ—distorted images will come from such things to flagellate you. All this I see, rejoicing yet suffering with you and for you!

How right you are too about "silence's speech." When we wish to be silent, God makes us speak, and vice versa. I, too, in a smaller measure, am even now on the horns of this dilemma! God is directing priests to Madonna House! This overwhelms me, whilst it transports me with joy, too!

Yet I cannot understand it. For in my wildest dreams I never imagined that when a tiny Lay Apostolate started 33 years ago in a tiny store front on a slummy street in Toronto it would draw PRIESTS to itself. We have 13 priests—4 resident, permanent ones, 9 associates, and one being ordained for MH May 31st. Can you credit this, beloved Fr. Louis? I barely can.

But this is not all. They say that they have been drawn through me! This I can only accept with difficulty, for it is so dark, this mystery. But I can accept it in faith: God uses weak instruments, etc. Also, perhaps, because of perseverance, becoming like earth plowed by it [perseverance] for such priestly seeds.

But now they want me to speak to them, to teach them the MH spirit. All I can do so far is to say, like the prophet of old, "Lord, I am a child and can say only ah, ah, ah!"

I am asked to speak where I have no words. You are silenced when your heart is full of words on war, peace. The world seems hungry to hear!

## Catherine de Hueck Doherty to Thomas Merton

*July 29, 1963*

Dear Father Louis,

It is always thus with us, you and me. You had written me November 12, 1962, exactly, and I am answering you on July 29, 1963. [Catherine seems to have forgotten her letter of May 8, 1963.] Yet, I know I do not have to apologize for the delay, because there really hasn't been a delay. You know and I know that I have answered your letter many times over, and that we have met; and in a manner of speaking, "discussed it" in many strange places, in many quiet places, where people who both try to love God and one another the way God wants them to, meet!

I knew you would be glad to hear about the Poustinya. I have been there and I am going there again, and hope I will go there often and for longer periods. I truly sense the need for solitude, for fasting, for silence, and for this type of prayer.

This need is like a hunger within me. At times it seems an all-consuming hunger that I cannot put into words, but that fills me, and in filling, reveals the emptiness that is in me. A strange emptiness that I do not quite understand and yet somehow understand. I think it comes from my poverty, the poverty of a creature that I realize so well. Perhaps it comes from the fact that as yet I must have a "small heart," though I pray to the Lord constantly to enlarge it. Maybe I am afraid of the pain that always comes "with that enlarging of His"!

Maybe, on the other hand, He, knowing my small heart, fills it just enough for me to empty it, or to give the gifts that He has laid in there to others. And then I have to go back to be replenished. Be that as it may, the hunger for the Poustinya periodically reaches strange and, at times, frightening proportions.

I do not visualize the Poustinya as a flight from the world. Well do I know enough facets of the mystery of evil to realize that there is danger in the Poustinya too, the danger of an almost psychosomatic desire to withdraw from the tension, the pressure, the "being eaten up by others." Yes, of this I am very well aware.

No, the Poustinya can be, as you know, I am sure, not a Poustinya, not a desert, but a sort of dreamy Shangri-La, if one goes there with the idea of withdrawal. I don't. And though I hunger for silence, solitude, fasting and prayer, I never hide from myself the fact that the Poustinya is also an encounter, or a place of encounter, with that Mystery of Evil. With the grace of God I must enter that miasmic, frightening darkness, there to wrestle for the very soul of the world, for the souls of all my brothers and sisters in Christ the world over.

Funny, Father Louis, that such an unimportant, weak person like myself should even write or think or dream of the paragraph that I have written above. I could easily say to myself—"Who in the hell do you think you are, Katie, that God will allow you, or give you, any graces or strength to wrestle with Satan at his powerful best." For he is that in the desert. He displays himself, preens himself. In a manner of speaking, the desert is his habitat.

Yet, I do not ask myself this question, because I enter into another mystery, the mystery of God's choice of the "weak and the simple." It begins there, in the desert, that terrible, awesome, incomprehensible, mysterious fight of man with the Mystery of Evil. I think that is the beginning of any Apostolate. It is in that intangible field in the desert that, by the grace of God, we get the strength to return to "the heat of the day," the market places of the world, the full contact with humanity. It is then that we become "the silver refined seven times in the furnace of God's making, the daggers of His love, the arrows of His tenderness, the bows of His compassion."

Far from evading our responsibility in the desert, if we approach it in fear and trembling, humility and the right reasons and motives, we learn there to face things; at least I must, because my apostolic life is definitely in the marketplaces of the world.

I had to smile at the ways of God with you, and the way you become silent, or you speak, and so on. And yet, a strange pain enters my soul too. I can reveal it to you because I know you will understand. The pain deals with your superiors, with all those who have eyes and see not, and ears and hear not.

You say the Church is slow in taking a definite position. I know you know how tragically slow its human elements are. I know you know all about the Negro situation now, for all things reach you, and all news jumps your cloistered walls faster than they enter our open doors.

One of the priests in the forefront of the battle in Washington is Fr. Geno Baroni.[18] We have a team in Aquia, 30 miles outside of Washington, in the "silent diocese of Bishop Russell." [Fr. Geno] is crucified on that silence. But I needn't go into the details. You know them all. From all sides we hear from the Negro about the tragic absence of the Church in the inter-racial field, which has ceased to be really inter-racial and never really was, but was simply a question of just charity and justice.

Yet, the Holy Ghost is again a Wind blowing through the Church. Pope John, and I hope and pray, Pope Paul, will open the doors of the Church wide. Pope John has done so. Now it is up to Pope Paul to open the doors and windows of the Church for that Wind of the Holy Ghost to blow through.

Yes, I agree with you. I too know by now a multitude of people who seek love and despair of finding it in our cold institutional gatherings. And I too am filled with admiration and love for those rough and tumble people and organizations who are fighting for peace. Yet, an indescribable pain fills my heart because the official announcements are so cold and so institutional.

Yes, I too wish you could come and talk these things over. But I am afraid you will not break the silence of our northern woods unless you came to our Poustinya, which is indeed deep, deep in the woods. For MH itself is a strange place, Father Louis, to which from all the corners of the North American continent, as well as from Asia, Africa and Europe, people come in search of that love you and I talk about.

Just take the last weeks of July and the month of August. We had a whole slew of young people graduated from high school, brought by a priest from Indiana. This week-end 20 seminarians are coming from a Canadian seminary. Next week a whole group of nurses on their way to foreign missions is stopping by. And the week after that, 50 university students from Montreal are going to have five extraordinary days of talking about God and love and foreign missions. And there will be Hindus and Mohammeadans, and all kinds of wondrous and strange people talking with us.

Someone recently remarked that Madonna House, Combermere, was the crossroads of the world. Everyone meets everyone here, or so it seems. Lay apostolic groups come and are replaced by others. Dialogues, conversations, hospitality, availability—all abide in MH. The neurotics and the non-neurotics come. Priests? We almost have lost track of why priests come. Perhaps because they find love, and Christ's hospitality, and intellectual and spiritual stimulation. I really wouldn't know except that they do come. Harlem, N.Y., frankly, looks a little tame to me at times, when I behold all the currents of the modern world meeting here in human form.

So, if you and I, or you and my spiritual family, were to have conversation, we would have to go to the Poustinya to have it.

How right you are, THE WORST THING IS THE FAILURE OF THE GOOD. This is what is really eating me up like a fire. What is it that you can do, Father Louis? What is it that you can become TO SET THE GOOD ONES ON FIRE WITH THE LOVE OF GOD? Listen to me, dearly beloved Father. It is a cry in the night, really, for my spiritual family is increasing, and they *are* good. But some spark, something is missing. What is it? How can I give it to them? How can our priests give it to them?

The darkness of hell encompasses me when I contemplate this fact. Reason tells me that it, too, is a mystery. But my Russian soul, so conditioned to look into itself, will not let me be. It keeps asking of me, constantly without ceasing, "What have you left undone in being or doing before the Lord, that those whom He has entrusted to you have not yet caught the fullness of His fire?" I do not ask you to answer me tomorrow, or the day after. Perhaps your prayers will bring me the answer on their silent wings. But I know that some day, somehow, in some manner, I will get that answer; and you will be the instrument that will give it to me.

I beg you to rejoice with us of Madonna House, for the Lord has certainly done marvels for us. A priest, Rev. Robert Pelton, has been ordained for us by our Bishop, on May 31 of this year. And so the impossible dream that I never dreamt—because I was sure that it was an impossibility—has come true. We not only have four priests in Madonna House; we not only have 10 associate priests; BUT WE HAVE ONE NEWLY ORDAINED JUST FOR THE APOSTOLATE. ALLELUIA! ALLELUIA! ALLELUIA!

You're constantly in my prayers. In fact, you are in them daily. I can read between lines, even as you can. And so I shall continue to pray, not that the pain, the fight, the temptations, the doubts be removed from you, but that God would give you the strength to know, really know, THAT HIS GRACE IS ENOUGH.

Lovingly yours in Mary, Catherine

## Catherine de Hueck Doherty to Thomas Merton

Pax Caritas

*November 15, 1964*

Dear Father Louis,

It has been a long time since I have written to you, but then speech is not always needed, on paper or otherwise, for people who love one another. But now I come to talk to you because I am unclear about God's ways with me. Which, of course, is not to be wondered at considering Who He is and who I am!

What do you make of the sudden influx, contacts, lunges that the old contemplative orders have suddenly (or is it?) developed toward the lay apostolate, and very specially to Madonna House, and strangely to me. For behold, living amongst us is Fr. Hilarion, a Trappist of Spencer, with full permission of his abbot. Fr. Walter, I think of your Abbey, passed 2–3 days here?! The Carmelites (men) bought 350 acres near us! 2 Carmelite nuns who left their order came here, seeking answers. Benedictines, even Camaldolese, have been inquiring, not to mention a tremendous influx of priests (order and secular). 634 have passed thru our doors since 1964.

But it is the contemplatives that seem to come seeking something I know not what, from Madonna House and me. Never has my utter poverty been so apparent to me. They seem to want to establish a hermetical life on the periphery [of Madonna House] yet also in depth in some way with us.

I am reminded of Russia where this was often done. They ask me about this. What can I tell them? They are so big, so learned before God. I stand in awe of them all. In them so clearly visible is the one immense priesthood of Christ! How does one tell such holy ones anything?

I speak like a child "ah, ah." Yes, I feel like speaking these words of the prophet. Contemplation to me is so very simple. It goes on all the time "inside" of me, because of love. It cannot be stopped because it is like a hunger, a fire, that burns inside of one. Once you have passionately fallen in love with God, contemplation becomes the very essence of you, while you go about the Father's business. Nothing interferes with it because it can't. Love unites with the Beloved thru it. It goes on amidst the noise of cities, the chaotic brouhas of lecture tours, the whirlwind of places, the swish of auto tires on thruways. In the slums, in the fine parlors, it is always there, for it is just simply and naturally the "being one with God" inside oneself. You see, He wants it, you wanted it, and there it is.

But all these wonderful priests, esp. Trappists and all, keep asking and asking. I get lost, answering, because I have not too much book knowledge about what they call "mystical ways." Oh, I have read books about it, but only a few make sense. Most are too complex for me.

Yet they are sincere, and I understand well what they want:

Silence—so they can have speech with men;

Solitude—so they can share it with men (its riches which is charity);

Penance—so they can heal men's souls. It is, we say in Russia, the wine and oil of the Good Samaritan to help the men besieged by robbers;

Prayer—so that they teach men to pray too;

Hospitality—to the poor and pilgrims especially;

Work—not only for themselves but with and for others.

This seems good to me, and very simple. But why are they so complex about it, as they seem to be about contemplation? I feel like an idiot, I confess. Will you help me to answer their questions (if I must?) please!

This morning I prayed for you intensely at Mass. Are you OK? You are soon going to be 50 years old, Father Louis. A good age. How wonderful that you have been allowed to help so many in such a short time. The Lord loves you much! I do too.

Yet I prayed today for peace for your turbulent heart!

Lovingly in Christ the great Revolutionary and Love, Catherine

## Thomas Merton to Catherine de Hueck Doherty

*November 21, 1964*

Dear Catherine,

. . . I have known for a long time that in the contemplative Orders of this country the accepted framework has not been adequate to take care of the vocations. The monasteries both of common life and of hermits (if one can call a hermit group a monastery) are organized in a rigid and stereotyped way for one kind of life only, which is not bad in its own way, and which seems to persist because it is relatively easy to keep in order. It is a matter of rules and observances which keep the monk busy and enable him to live a life of comparative recollection and prayer, protecting him against some of the distractions of life, keeping him in trim by a certain amount of austerity.

Unfortunately this regimented form of existence, which is sound enough when based on the best traditions, tends to be rather empty and frustrating, to many vocations, and indeed there is a very general feeling that the life easily becomes a dead end. It retains its meaning for those who have some kind of responsibility in the community or who work in a way that contributes to the community, while for others, well, they tend to vegetate. There are few real contemplatives who can continue simply to live the monastic life as it is organized and really *grow* as they go on. The older generation still manages it. The younger ones, after my age group, tend to be more and more dissatisfied and disoriented.

There is no question that the hermit life is a legitimate and traditional development of the monastic vocation. Simply to block this off and forbid it has kept the question from being raised in the past. It can no longer be kept out of sight. I think in fact that in the monastic Orders we are going to frankly face the need of allowing temporary or permanent hermitages for some of our members. And in fact I already have a dacha or something, which I suppose is somewhat like yours, though perhaps bigger because it was originally built to house groups of ministers coming for dialogue. They go there to converse with us, not to live there. It is a three-room cottage, very simple.

There is also a very keen sense of need for a simpler, more "open" type of monastic life, in which the work will be more "real" and there will be more sense that one is living as ordinary poor people live, not as institutionalized and dressed-up "poor monks" with personal poverty in a rich community. This is one of the great trends in the Order today. It is shaking the Order up quite a bit, especially in Europe. There we have Dutch monks who want to go out and work in factories. Their aspiration is good but the way of fulfilling it seems to me to be off the track. At least for monks.

You say they come to you with all sorts of complicated questions. Yes, that is true. They have been reading and hearing all sorts of things, and in many cases they may be, though smart, spiritually confused. The basic trouble is perhaps that they are still very immature in the spiritual life, because they are very centered on a "self" for which they want to attain the best of ends: they want to possess "contemplation" and "God." But to think contemplation is something that one can "attain" and "possess" is just to get off on the wrong road from the very beginning. What they really need is solid and simple direction, and more than that, what they need is the kind of really basic sort of training that the Desert Fathers and the early monasteries gave: to shut up and stop all their speculation and get down to living a simple laborious life in which they forget themselves. I am sure that around Madonna House you can help them find a more authentic and realistic simplicity than they may have had in monasteries.

As for the "hermit," well, the danger is that there is no precedent among us and no one to lead the way. It would be a great shame if what I think to be a genuine movement proceeding from God would in fact be discredited by a lot of false and immature hermits trying it out and making a mess of it. I would say that very probably at Madonna House you could really be of service to two or three mature and trained monks with a capacity to be hermits . . .

My advice in the concrete would be to have a couple of hermitages, or three near Madonna House, and allow well-tested men to try out there temporarily, say for Lent, or for three months in summer, etc., and see what develops . . .

I must close now. I am involved in this myself, and have definite hopes of living in a hermitage here in the woods sometime in the not too distant future. In fact I do spend much time there already, and sleep there, etc. I am sure it can all be worked out very simply and quietly, but unfortunately people have a mania for organization and complication, trying to draw up detailed programs for everything all the time, and they forget to just live. I hope they will just let me get out there and live with God and work things out in a simple practical way as time goes on, instead of making up a rigid and legalistic set of rules. However, I will take whatever my Superiors see fit to impose . . .

Most cordially, Tom Merton

## Catherine de Hueck Doherty to Thomas Merton

PAX CARITAS

*December 16, 1965*

Dearly Beloved Fr. Louis,

What shall I say, this week before Christmas, to you whom my heart loves? Perhaps share with you my meditation. So I enclose it herewith. It is a letter to my spiritual children, but I know you can read between the lines, and that you will get out of it that which I cannot tell you in words.

We do not write to each other often, but when my soul wants to speak to someone who understands it, I sit down and write you a letter. I am doing so at this time because my soul is in a sort of agony, and I know that yours is too. Love, not knowing space or time, intuitively senses things that cannot be really spoken in words.

My soul is in agony and I am filled with fears. I, who seldom know fear, fear for the Church, for the people of God, like Staretz Silouan of the *Undistorted Image,* that I am sure you have read. And, according to the ways of my people, "I weep over the world."

Every week Catholic newspapers (as well as some secular ones) bring news of priests who are silenced. Just in the last two weeks, as you probably know, two Jesuits in New Jersey, Fr. Dan Berrigan of New York, a Franciscan priest in Albany, N.Y., another in California. I don't even mention the Los Angeles ones. Their "sin"? They helped the poor, they stood for racial equality, for love of all men. They helped strikers, they bucked corrupt city political machines, they did what Christ bade us do.

Trappists, Franciscans, Carmelites, Jesuits, and many other Orders, whose members pass constantly through Madonna House, are seething with turmoil. There are wars in Vietnam, but there are deeper Wars in the souls of men.

The New Breed, who came to Madonna House last summer, is a strange combination of honesty, integrity and emotional hostilities that are almost as dangerous a mixture for the spirit as an atom bomb for the body. Dorothy Day is in the limelight adversely and positively. People burn themselves, kill themselves, for peace. And people kill other people because they believe in love, in peace and in God.

The Vatican Council opens many windows, and hope springs in human hearts. Then again I behold the sight of hope being crushed. Can anyone hear that sound? It has a sound, you know, a terrible sound, like a death knell, like a dirge. Can anyone hear that sound and live? Yes, I hear it and I do live. Madonna House is like a chalice, and so is my heart, that is filled to the brim with the hunger of man for God, with man's searching, man's yearning and man's despair.

Fr. Francis Martin of the monastery of Spencer is with us. You know him, I am sure. He is a biblical scholar, a young man of 35, very brilliant. Like all of us here, he too is in the winepress.

Are our garments died red? Are we the man from Bosra? I don't know.

All I know is that my soul is in agony, even as yours is, and I knock at your door, the Russian pilgrim, weary, begging the alms of a place to rest in spirit, begging the alms of your tenderness and your love and your understanding heart. For, you see, underneath it all, I still have peace and joy somewhere deep. Will you help me to open the doors that hide them, so that I might see? For peace and joy are the reflection of God's face in glory, and all I traffic with these days is the man in whom there is no comeliness. Yet, with all this, I come to you, knowing that we will be together at His crib, and behold a sign of God's promise fulfilled, which is our joy. This is a sort of incoherent letter, but that's the way it came to me, and that's the way I send it off.

Lovingly yours in Mary, Catherine

P.S. Eddie sends his love too. Why don't you get out for a little while? Do they let you out these days? And spend some time in our poustinia—desert—hidden away in a forest on a mountain too.

## Thomas Merton to Catherine de Hueck Doherty

*His last letter to Catherine.*

*January 12, 1966*

Dear Catherine,

I have been wanting to answer your Christmas letter and your Advent anguish. It is probably gone now, unless the Lord has been keeping you in it as He sometimes does. Living in the hermitage permanently now I am learning the ways of anguish better and the ways of tears too, but also I am taking myself in hand about it, because I am coming to realize that there is a subtle way in which the world grips us and will not set us free: for we must realize that the tyranny of worldly power today holds people precisely by continual anguish and torments them with insecurity, in order every day to get a little better grip. That is the demonic thing about this cold war and hot war and the ceaseless news . . . One must weep for the world, like Staretz Silouane, whom I love as you do. One must even, as he did, keep our souls in "hell" without despairing. But also we must gradually get so that the world and its rule of terror does not reach in to try to dominate our inner soul.

That is why with the business of Dan Berrigan, for example, it is not so great a reason for anguish as one might at first sight think and Dorothy [Day] in the *Catholic Worker* I think is quite right when she says it was perhaps a good thing for him to be shipped out. As far as I know, the authentic story is this: it is not as simple as those protesting against it have made it out to be. Rather his Provincial is a fairly good sort, is trying to be broadminded and open, and is generally loosening things up, but there were fears in the province that because of Dan the General might descend on the Provincial and spoil everything. Thus (and I don't doubt the Chancery had a hand in it) it was thought wise to smuggle Dan out for a while (I know him very well). Actually, the uproar was justified in the sense that, taking Dan as an occasion, people simply expressed their disgust once for all with the "old way" of doing things, a way which has in any case been deplored by the Council itself. Hence, on this occasion, people simply began to vent their wrath on this particular Superior indeed, but aiming at *all* Superiors who have habitually and flagrantly abused their power for years, consistently tricking and circumventing subjects, never frank with them, always trusting them in a way that is an implicit insult to the dignity of the Christian person, and so on. The lid had to come off at last and it did. I am sure there will be more of the same, and there is no indication that there can be any really widespread change without it. The old ways are established and I suppose that most people just seem to think they are the right ways and there can be no other. Well, the Church will never wake up unless there is a change in this also, as in the Holy Office (I bet it will take time for that one to change too). Thank heaven there are plenty of good Superiors too, who are open-minded and ask for nothing better than to give their subjects some initiative especially in things like race relations. I am sure there is no question of impeding Dan Berrigan in this regard: it is the "pacifism" that is the trouble, in Cardinal Spellman's bailiwick.[19]

I thought it might be useful to say these things, as we are going to have more and more of these same alarms. Let us pray for one another to grow in hope and freedom and do so precisely in and by that anguish which is really a great good though we would certainly prefer any other at the time it is with us . . . I was very anguished myself over Roger La Porte's burning himself alive and had a six weeks' struggle with the peace people I am associated with, Dorothy included, but we came out all right, and I think we have all profited by it.[20] Some tried to make out that Roger was a martyr, but in fact I think he was a kind of sign of judgment, in his well-intentioned confusion, something to teach the Catholic peace movement that there is something far more important than just getting coverage in the press and on TV.

Well, we won't really get out of the wilderness until everything is pressed out and there is nothing left but the pure wine to be offered to the Lord, transubstantiated into His Blood. Let us look forward to that day when we will be entirely in Him and He in us and the Father in and over all. Then there will be true peace which the world cannot give . . .

Cordially always in Christ, fr. m. Louis

*Catherine de Hueck Doherty to Fr. Flavian, O.C.S.O., Abbot, Abbey of Gethsemani, on the occasion of Merton's death.*

PAX CARITAS

*December 12, 1968*

Dearly Beloved Father and Friend,

Thank you for your telegram. Father Louis, in some strange mysterious way I never quite understood, was in part my spiritual son.

As a Christian my heart sings an Alleluia, for Father corresponded with me through the years. And as the years went by his hunger for meeting the God he loved so much could be read between the lines.

So my heart sings an Alleluia. But in a manner of speaking it is a strange Alleluia. It is made up of unshed tears. And tears are like shining jewels when the sun strikes them. And the sun of joy is in my Alleluia.

The world has lost a great man. Monasticism has lost a great man. But all of us, and I say this in all simplicity of heart, have gained a saint.

When I received your telegram yesterday it was just before Mass time. Each of our ten priests of Madonna House is going to say many Masses for the repose of Father Louis' soul. But the news of his death came, as I said, before the Mass I attended, the Mass of Our Lady, and he was part of it.

As yet, I have not absorbed completely the news of his birthday in the Lord, but somehow I feel him intensely close to me these last 24 hours. If there be any communication of this type, closeness of this type, then I have to say that it is one of joy.

Forgive this somewhat incoherent, semi-dramatic letter. What are human words before the mystery of life and death, the mystery of love, of gain and of loss. Faith sings its Alleluia. Flesh brings unshed tears. Love transcending space and time reveals the secret of the communion of saints.

So I'll end my letter with deep gratitude to you, dearly beloved Father, for your telegram, for it is evident that you knew how much I loved Father Louis, and what he meant to me. I thank you for your tender and compassionate understanding, and strangely enough, as often happens with my beloved Trappists, I am with you in your Monastery sharing your pain and your joy.

Gratefully and sincerely yours in Mary, Catherine

# IV. CATHERINE'S TALK ON THE OCCASION OF MERTON'S DEATH

[Merton] had died sometime before 3 p.m. Bangkok time. A telegram was sent that night to Gethsemani. Crossing the International Date Line, it arrived some fourteen hours after his death, at 10 a.m. on December 10, at the monastery. The tenth of December, 1968, was, to the day, the twenty-seventh anniversary of Thomas Merton's arrival at the Monastery of Our Lady of Gethsemani.

Michael Mott
*The Seven Mountains of Thomas Merton* (568–69)

*Catherine's letter to Fr. Flavian (p. 89) was written on December 12. She must have been one of the first people contacted by Fr. Flavian. He knew of her special relationship with Merton. On December 13, in a letter to Karl Stern (the famous psychiatrist and longtime friend of Catherine's), Catherine wrote, "We all mourn the death of Thomas Merton. The Abbot of Gethsemani wired me about it. It is a great loss to monasticism and to the world, but my heart sings an Alleluia, for I know how Father Louis hungered to meet the God he loved so much."*

*At Madonna House, Catherine regularly had spiritual reading every day after lunch. Often she would read from some book, and then make comments. At the spiritual reading on December 11 one of the Madonna House priests, Fr. Briere, read excerpts from* The Seven Storey Mountain. *Catherine interspersed some personal reflections.*

*Since her comments that day came some twenty-seven years after Merton's Harlem visit, I don't relate them as presenting any kind of strict historical accuracy: They were the reflections of a seventy-two year old, speaking off the cuff about someone she loved deeply. It's an example of how Catherine spoke to us about the events of her life in the apostolate.*

*Catherine had a great imagination. Especially when speaking publicly, she was more intent on keeping the interest of her audience and avoiding putting them to sleep with a dull historical or theological lecture. Her public speaking—I can testify—was always interesting.*

## Talk by Catherine at Spiritual Reading

[Merton] came to visit us. He was slightly shook-up. He left and came back. There is a picture of me that he took in a restaurant which is sold in the PX in the summer. I wear braids and a Russian kerchief. The restaurant was much too swanky for my outfit, but neither of us cared. He was a gourmet; he liked wine, women and song. We had a very good dinner with wine and so forth. He was telling me about poverty and chastity and obedience, and about the love of God and St. Francis as only Thomas Merton could talk, even in his youth.

I got very tired of the conversation because, first, I didn't want to go to the restaurant; secondly, I don't like steak; and thirdly, we were supposed to be going some place and this was delaying us, this long and beautiful harangue. So I said, "Why don't you shut up for a while?"

He looked at me because nobody had ever told him to shut up before. He was so stunned that he almost choked on a piece of something. He said, "Why should I shut up?" I said, "Because you talk and you don't do anything. You are grand at talking about God. Why don't you stop all this damn nonsense of steaks and wine and women and dreams of holy poverty? Why don't you come and spend some time in Harlem, like three months, or six months, or a year? Maybe then you will get some sense about these things and then you can talk about them."

He said, "Now that's an idea." So he ruminated on that for quite a while. Then one day he telephoned me and said, "I'm coming." I said, "Now that is the first sensible thing you did so far." I knew very little about his background which he wrote in *Seven Storey Mountain*. I take people as they are: "There was a professor, and his name was Thomas Merton; and he was talking big, see." That's all I knew about him.

So he arrived. Well, I had met his friend Bob Lax before that. They were great friends. Bob Lax was a Hasidic Jew, one of the holy sects of the Jews who observe all the rites of the Jews. He was a poet. He was teaching poetry at Bonaventure, and he was writing poetry for the *New York Times*. He was making big money. His family was from Olean. They had a hotel, and boy did they have a hotel! They took me there for one of those gourmet meals.

I gave Bob Lax a mop once to mop the floor, and about half an hour later no Bob Lax. So I crossed the street and there was Bob Lax. He had a

*Catherine's Talk on the Occasion of Merton's Death*    93

pail of water, and he just sloshed it all over the room, standing peacefully in the water, wetting his shoes. The mop was dry. He was writing a beautiful poem on washing floors! I said, "You can't write a poem on this unless you finish the job, or it is not existentialistic." But he said, "I never washed a floor." I said, "Alright, why didn't you say so. I will show you how." So you see what my problem was with those very holy people.

Well, Thomas Merton was like that. When I gave him a mop he looked at it, looked again, and said, "I imagine it's connected with the floor." I'm not going into a thousand anecdotes about how Thomas Merton had the Negroes rolling in the aisles when he was dusting, or mopping or something. But things were going along fine. He even said one day, "I think I will try to wear second-hand clothes from the second-hand room." He was very well tailored, you know. He had money of his own. He had been in France and Europe and so forth. I said, "That's a good idea for a person like you." We were getting along fine. I mean, he was learning about faith, and about poverty.

It's quite a story, when he was bitten by his first bedbug. He arrived! We had this chart: "How many bedbugs did you kill sleeping last night?" He or she who had the most got the first donation of cigarettes. People would come in and give us a pack of cigarettes. Thomas Merton came in and said, "I found a bedbug in my room." We put on the chart: "Thomas Merton, 1 bedbug, no cigarette." I managed thirty-five to forty, and Flewy [one of the staff workers] came second; but we discounted ten or fifteen because we were fatter than everybody else. So we said, "Yeh, that's the way people live around here."

He kept writing poems, and seemingly he was getting the idea of a vocation.

One day Father Furfey gave us a retreat. He was my spiritual director; he was head of the Sociological Department at Catholic University. He gave us one of the most beautiful retreats on the Lay Apostolate, on the people of God. He used those words, which we are using now after Vatican II. Thomas Merton was sitting there, lost in the words of Father Furfey.

Two days later he said, "Catherine, I have found my vocation." I said, "Hurray!" He said, "I am going to be a Trappist." To this day I have never understood how it was possible that a retreat given on the lay apostolate clarified his vocation to the contemplative life! But it did, and so he departed. But he left me a book, his autobiography [*The Secular Journal*]. He inscribed it, "I have learned much in Friendship House and I want to leave you this book. Take it. If you sell it you get the royalties because I am not going to write any more in the Trappists."

Well, we have his photograph. Put it on the table with his books so that people can read them if they want to. But you see how deeply, in a sense, he enters into our lives. I will bring out his correspondence and maybe we can read a few excerpts from it. There are some very beautiful passages about many things. We corresponded through the years. You know that he was seeking a poustinia. Finally his superior allowed him to live in one. He was so happy about that.

So, a great friend is home at last! He has given up everything, and he has received everything, so let us rejoice.

# AFTERWORD

I owe much to Catherine.

*The Secular Journal of Thomas Merton*

I am the postulator for the cause of canonization for Catherine. Postulators gather material for the Church's discernment regarding a person's heroic living of the gospel. One aspect of holiness concerns how a person *inspired others* to love the Lord. Such influence is another indication of the love of God working through her or him. My "postulator's hat" nudges me, at the end of this presentation of their friendship, to pose the question of Catherine's impact on Merton. It is my conviction that Catherine had a strong and life-changing influence on him. I begin by presenting several eyewitness accounts about what happened to him as a result of his relationship with Catherine.

Betty Schneider, an early volunteer in Friendship House, was in Harlem with Merton. She told me, in a conversation, that Merton was vastly influenced by Catherine. Peggy Parsons was also in Harlem when Merton was there. In a personal communication to me, this is how she summed up Catherine's effect on Merton: "By the grace of the Holy Spirit, Catherine entered into Thomas Merton's life at just the right moment. She understood where Merton was coming from in his spiritual aspirations. For Merton, as also for Bob Lax, Catherine's vocation and pursuit of a radical Christian witness to the world illuminated the way for them. There was no uncertainty in Catherine: She comprehended the world we lived in, and the role of the Christian and of the Church in that world."

Stanley Vishnewski was a friend of both Catherine and Dorothy Day in the early years, and he had met Merton in Harlem. He wrote a book on the Catholic Worker, *Wings of the Dawn*. In a chapter on Friendship House he wrote: "The spiritual zeal of the early FH staff workers was contagious. Many a lukewarm Catholic came there for the social life, and was soon caught up in the Love of God. Tom Merton was one who found his vocation working with the 'B'" (p. 154).

It was the zeal exploding from Catherine's great heart that was the source of this contagion. As Merton was led to the Trappists, so too a number of people were led to the religious or the priestly life because of their FH experience. As one of the outstanding Christians of the twentieth century, her inspiration of Merton is another testimony to her holiness. Only great souls can affect great souls.

Paul Pearson, of the Merton Center at Bellarmine College, Kentucky, told me that it wasn't until 1963 that Merton started to keep all his letters. Before then, he only kept letters he had written to "important" people. Catherine was one of these. When I asked Paul what he thought Catherine meant to Merton, he said: "I think she was certainly very important in the discernment of his vocation and he felt she was one of his 'spiritual parents' so to speak."

This theme that I have chosen for my afterword—"What was Catherine's influence on Thomas Merton?"—is rather elusive. Even though we know a fair amount about their relationship through their letters presented in this book, still, a certain question remains: "What exactly did she *mean* to Merton?" In his preface to *The Secular Journal* he has some reflections on his relationship with Catherine. Towards the end he writes: "I owe much to Catherine." What exactly did he *owe* her?

Did he consider her, in that crucial year of 1941, as a sort of "spiritual mother," a "spiritual parent," as Pearson suggests? In Catherine's letter to the Abbot upon Merton's death (p. 89), she says, "Father Louis, in some strange mysterious way I never quite understood, was in part my spiritual son."

Was this understanding of their relationship mutual: Did Merton consider Catherine *his* spiritual mother? She was nineteen years his senior. Is that old enough to be a spiritual mother? In reading their correspondence, I couldn't get any sense that he did consider her a spiritual mother to him. Could such a relationship on his part have been in his heart, but unexpressed? Possibly. In 1941 he certainly sought and trusted her spiritual guidance about his vocation. But, it seems, not later on: in the letters to Catherine in this book he mostly shares his own spiritual and theological insights, and does not really ask her opinion—much less guidance—on personal matters.

In a letter to him in 1963 (p. 74) she wrote: "You know, of course, that I love you much in the Lord. For it was He Who brought us together in FH for such a short spell of time. In a strange manner I feel like an older sister or even mother to you. Why? I cannot tell. Maybe it isn't even that at all—yet there is a bond."

An "older sister" then? Perhaps. He didn't have a sister, and so might have thought it nice to have a "spiritual" one.

In Catherine's letter of February 17, 1958 (p. 47), she expresses her own multifaceted relationship to Merton in this way: "I have never thought of you as a celebrity. I guess you are a big one at that; but to me, in a manner of speaking, you are a son. And in another sense, a Father. And in a third, a brother. And together we seek our Beloved."

The age of a priest meant little to Catherine. Her strong faith saw every priest as Father. So to think of Merton as Father Louis was not unusual. Catherine had two younger brothers, so it would have been easy to see Merton as another brother.

But her last statement, I believe, is the key to their friendship: "Together we seek our Beloved." They saw their relationship as a common thirsting for sanctity, and this is one of the major themes in their correspondence.

For example, in her first letter to him (October 14, 1941): "Out of this comes the right results in the line of politics, and so on. Yes, it means a Saint, or trying to become one. Yet, it also means teaching others politics, writing for magazines, speaking and teaching, because a Saint (as all things of God) is a well-rounded person, ready and able to do what God wants him to do. And that might be some or all of the above. Charity is simply part and parcel of the Saint because its other name is LOVE. And one cannot be a Saint and wield the above weapons unless that foundation is ready. But never separate sainthood from ordinary living. For, after all, what is it fundamentally but doing everyday things extremely well." And another example: "Well, I don't know. It certainly isn't the autobiography of the Little Flower. And you may not be a saint now. But who can tell, perhaps you or even I will someday be a saint. With God's mercy, all things are possible! I surely will pray" (February 17, 1958).

We at Madonna House heard Catherine quote many times that famous saying of Leon Bloy: "There is but one tragedy, not to be a saint."

Thirty years before Vatican II's teaching that everyone is called to holiness, to the perfection of charity, Catherine was preaching that everyone is called to sanctity. This was the inspiration for all of her guidance and instruction: she had a great desire to be a saint herself, and she wanted to help others along that path.

In these letters of Merton we have read: "When you get right down to it, Catholic Action means . . . first of all being a saint"; "when it comes to saving souls, the first thing of all is our own sanctification"; and "His providence certainly designed a rough age for us to be saints in. So let us pray that we will get there; or you, who are on the way, pray for me who have been seven years starting and not getting very far. But I like it anyway." He entered Gethsemani because he believed it would be the best place for him to become a saint.

But at the heart of what I believe was the effect of Catherine upon Merton—what he "owed her"—was something that happened to others as well: young Tom encountered in Catherine a woman who was really *in love with God,* spoke about God with passion and intimacy as if she really *knew* God, and lived the gospel in a profoundly incarnational way among the poor. By her life and teaching she manifested what it was to be—as she often put it—*in love with Jesus Christ.* Many people had their lives permanently and deeply changed by having met her. In short, *they had met a saint,* whether they knew it or not. Merton knew it.

There is a passage in Merton's autobiography where he puts into the minds and hearts of two Friars what he surmises they were experiencing about the power of Catherine's personality. I believe here he is expressing *his own* more mature understanding of what happened *to him* as a result of his meeting with Catherine. After several years of reflection on Catherine's influence on him in 1941, his comments in *The Seven Storey Mountain* contain, perhaps, even more penetrating insights into the impact she had on him. Time can often provide deeper perceptions to past experiences.

Merton and the two Friars had gone to pick up Catherine in Buffalo, New York:

> We were in a restaurant having something to eat, and the Baroness was talking about priests, and about the spiritual life and gratitude, and the ten lepers in the Gospel, of whom only one returned to give thanks to Christ for having cured them. She had made what seemed to me to be certainly a good point. But I suddenly noticed that it had struck the two Friars like a bombshell.

Then I realized what was going on. She was preaching to them. Her visit to St. Bonaventure's was to be, for them and the Seminarians and the rest who heard her, a kind of a mission, or a retreat. I had not grasped, before, how much this was part of her work; priests and religious had become, indirectly, almost as important a mission field for her as Harlem. It is a tremendous thing, the economy of the Holy Ghost! When the Spirit of God finds a soul in which He can work, He uses that soul for any number of purposes: opens out before its eyes a hundred new directions, multiplying its works and its opportunities for the apostolate almost beyond belief and certainly far beyond the ordinary strength of a human being.

Here was this woman who had started out to conduct a more or less obscure work helping the poor in Harlem, now placed in such a position that the work which had barely been begun was drawing to her souls from every part of the country, and giving her a sort of unofficial apostolate among the priesthood, the clergy and the religious Orders.

What was it that she had to offer them that they did not already possess? One thing: she was full of the love of God; and prayer and sacrifice and total, uncompromising poverty had filled her soul with something which, it seemed, these two men had often looked for in vain in the dry and conventional and merely learned retreats that fell to their lot. And I could see that they were drawn to her by the tremendous spiritual vitality of the grace that was in her, a vitality which brought with it a genuine and lasting inspiration, because it put their souls in contact with God as a living reality. And that reality, that contact, is something which we all need: and one of the ways in which it has been decreed that we should arrive at it, is by hearing one another talk about God. *Fides ex auditu.* And it is no novelty for God to raise up saints who are not priests to preach to those who are priests—witness the Baroness's namesake, Catherine of Siena. (pp. 357–58)

I believe Merton here is expressing the effect of Catherine *on him* during that trip in 1941.

Merton's appreciation of Catherine is expressed in another passage from *The Seven Storey Mountain,* in which he reflects on his first encounter with Catherine in Olean in 1941. Here I believe he is once again expressing Catherine's influence on *himself.* He, along with the Sisters and clergy at St.

Bonaventure's, was "being moved deeply" and "hearing the pure Franciscan ideal, the pure essence of the Franciscan apostolate":

> The Baroness was born a Russian. She had been a young girl at the time of the October Revolution. She had seen half of her family shot, she had seen priests fall under the bullets of the Reds, and she had escaped from Russia the way it is done in the movies, but with all the misery and hardship which the movies do not show, and none of the glamour which is their specialty.
>
> The experiences she had gone through, instead of destroying her faith, intensified and deepened it until the Holy Ghost planted fortitude in the midst of her soul like an unshakable rock. I never saw anyone so calm, so certain, so peaceful in her absolute confidence in God.
>
> Catherine de Hueck is a person in every way big: and the bigness is not merely physical: it comes from the Holy Ghost dwelling constantly within her, and moving her in all that she does.
>
> When she was working in that laundry, down somewhere near Fourteenth Street, and sitting on the curbstone eating her lunch with the other girls who worked there, the sense of her own particular vocation dawned upon her. It was the call to an apostolate, not new, but so old that it is as traditional as that of the first Christians: an apostolate of a laywoman in the world, among workers, herself a worker, and poor: an apostolate of personal contacts, of word and above all of example. There was to be nothing special about it, nothing that savored of a religious Order, no special rule, no distinctive habit. She, and those who joined her, would simply be poor—there was no choice on that score, for they were that already—but they would embrace their poverty, and the life of the proletariat in all its misery and insecurity and dead, drab monotony. They would live and work in the slums, lose themselves, in the huge anonymous mass of the forgotten and the derelict, for the only purpose of living the complete, integral Christian life in that environment—loving those around them, sacrificing themselves for those around them, and spreading the Gospel and the truth of Christ most of all by being saints, by living in union with Him, by being full of His Holy Ghost, His charity.
>
> As she spoke of these things, in that Hall, and to all these nuns and clerics, she could not help but move them all deeply, because what they were hearing—and it was too patent to be missed—was

nothing but the pure Franciscan ideal, the pure essence of the Franciscan apostolate of poverty, without the vows taken by the Friars Minor. And, for the honor of those who heard her, most of them had the sense and the courage to recognize this fact, and to see that she was, in a sense, a much better Franciscan than they were. She was, as a matter of fact, in the Third Order, and that made me feel quite proud of my own scapular, which was hiding under my shirt: it reminded me that the thing was not altogether without meaning or without possibilities! (pp. 342–43)

Perhaps the last public tribute Merton paid to Catherine was in his preface to *The Secular Journal.* He had had ten more years to reflect on who Catherine was since writing *The Seven Storey Mountain.* He wrote:

Since this work [*The Secular Journal*], and any royalties it may earn, belong to Catherine de Hueck Doherty's "Madonna House," it might be well to introduce the reader to both the foundress and her foundation. Baroness Catherine de Hueck fled from Russia when the Reds took over in 1917. She was still only a child. When I first met her her friends still called her "the Baroness" or more familiarly "B." Readers of *The Seven Storey Mountain* will remember her under this name. The title of nobility has since vanished into oblivion, and rightly. Never on the face of this earth was there anyone *less* of an effete aristocrat than Catherine. Her boundless, earthly solidity and her deep faith are those of a peasant. I always remember her as one of the most energetic and generous people I have ever met— and one of the most simple. Everything she says and does is quite direct, and she never pulls any of her punches. She goes straight to the heart of the issue. The revolution had made her poor. Far from resenting the fact, she embraced it with prodigious good humor and fervent thanksgiving as a marvelous grace from God. She resolved to make poverty her vocation with a vigor and directness that are thoroughly Franciscan.

She is not the kind of person that gets overexcited at the thought of communism. The Reds do not upset her, and never will. She has lived for forty years as a proletarian and she can size up communism with the shrewd common sense of the worker of the western world who has learned that not everything that comes out of Russia is necessarily good or necessarily evil. She knows that if there was a revolution in Russia, there were reasons for one: she has not ceased to believe in cause and effect, just because the revolution happened to enter, quite brutally, into her own personal life. She knows from experience why communism to some extent appeals to certain elements in the western working class, and to some extent repels them. Above all, because she is a Christian, she is thoroughly aware of the futility and inner contradictions of a dialectic that is purely materialistic. The Reds do not worry her, because she knows that they will end up in another one of those ash-cans, further down the street of history.

But at the same time, she is one who feels that Christianity cannot and must not be a mere matter of fine words and pretty speeches at Communion breakfasts. She knows that it is the business of Christians to point out the fallacy of communism not merely by their words, but by their lives: and this is not merely a matter of one's personal virtues, but of social conscience. Our duty as Christians does not end with the salvation of our own souls. We are debtors not only to God but to our neighbor, and Jesus Himself made it very clear that our neighbor is not just the one who lives in the apartment next door. The Parable of the Good Samaritan teaches us that everyone who suffers, everyone who is unjustly treated, who is oppressed, cheated, forgotten, or neglected, is our neighbor. And we have to love him as we love ourselves. It is no good to pass by on the other side of the road with our eyes devoutly cast down, with our lips murmuring pious prayers—and with plenty of money jingling in our pockets. More than that, Catherine is one who realizes more clearly than almost anyone I know, that her neighbor is not only her neighbor but he is also Christ. To love, serve and help our brother, is to love, serve and help Christ. She is one to whom the doctrine of the Mystical Body is something more than a stimulating theory.

This was one of the things she learned when she was working in a laundry and sharing her meager lunch with a fellow worker, as they sat together on the steps of a dingy brownstone house, in a New York slum district in the twenties. This was what moved her to start Friendship House, in Toronto, in 1930. This, too, was what brought her to Harlem in 1938, with nothing but a couple of dollars and a typewriter. She moved into a tenement on 135th Street, and Friendship House had entered the United States! . . .

When I was writing some of the final pages of this diary in 1941, I was on the point of joining Catherine de Hueck at Friendship House.

She had asked me to come, and the decision had been provisionally taken—until it became clear that my vocation lay elsewhere: in a Cistercian monastery. Nevertheless, I owe much to Catherine, and I am glad that this book can help Madonna House in some way. . . . (pp. ix–xii; xiv)

Of course, *I* can't call Catherine a saint yet! Postulators can't do that. But Merton believed that he had met one in Catherine. This is what he *owed* her. Catherine called saints "walking gospels." In 1941 Merton was *reading* about the saints—Theresa of Lisieux, John of the Cross, Francis of Assisi, Theresa of Avila. He was *reading* about them. It is my opinion that in Catherine de Hueck *he met his first saint.* After finishing Henri Gheon's book on the Little Flower, Merton said he was "knocked out by it completely" (*RM,* 431). In that spiritually charged and crucial year of 1941, I believe he was knocked out by Catherine!

# Notes

1. See Robert Wild, ed., *Comrades Stumbling Along: The Friendship of Catherine de Hueck Doherty and Dorothy Day as Revealed through Their Letters* (Staten Island, NY: Alba House, 2009).

2. "Catholic Action" was a term used to designate both a concept and a movement that flourished from the late nineteenth century to the first half of the twentieth century. In general, the term referred to organized lay activity aimed at Christianizing human society through nonpolitical works, in cooperation with the Church's hierarchy. Catholic Action was actively encouraged by several popes, especially Pius XI (1922–1939). The term passed out of use after Vatican II.

3. Rev. Hubert Vechierello, O.F.M., was head of the Science department and professor of Biology at St. Bonaventure.

4. The Jocists (Fr., Jeunesse Ouvrière Chrétienne, "Young Christian Workers") were a Catholic Action movement founded in Belgium by Cardinal Joseph Cardijin (d. 1967) shortly after World War I. The movement spread through Europe, then moved to Canada and the United States. Jocists encouraged their lay members to see the workplace as an opportunity for evangelization.

5. António de Oliveira Salazar (1889–1970), Portuguese economist who served as Prime Minister of Portugal for thirty-six years (1932–1968). As a young man, Salazar was a member of an elite group of Catholic

intellectuals in Portugal, and his rule was influenced by Catholic and papal thought.

6. Mary Jerdo, a Friendship House lay volunteer whom Merton befriended during his time in Harlem.

7. Joyce Kilmer (1886–1918), American poet and lecturer. A Catholic convert, Kilmer was killed in combat in France in World War I.

8. *A Thousand Shall Fall*, by Hans Habe. Published in 1941, the book is Habe's account of the fall of France in World War II, which he witnessed as a soldier in the French army.

9. "It is now generally known that the 'scandal' referred to was the fact that, while at Cambridge University, Merton fathered a child. Merton's guardian, Tom Bennett, made arrangements to care for the mother and child" (Shannon, *The Hidden Ground of Love*, 9).

10. Fr. Paul Hanly Furfey (1896–1992), professor of Sociology at Catholic University of America and chair of the department from 1932 to 1962. A prolific author and lecturer, he was deeply committed to social justice issues. He was Catherine's spiritual director at the time of this letter.

11. Robert Lax (1915–2000), poet, Catholic convert, and close friend of Merton's, the two having met at Columbia University in the 1930s. Lax spent a year at Friendship House in Harlem.

12. Naomi Burton Stone (d. 2004), Merton's literary agent and close friend.

13. Merton's complimentary words toward Catherine in his preface to *The Secular Journal* are included in the afterword of this book.

14. "Original Child Bomb," a prose-poem about the dropping of the atomic bomb on Hiroshima, originally published in 1961 in the magazine *PAX*.

15. Fr. John LaFarge, S.J. (1880–1963), American Jesuit priest, journalist, and promoter of interracial justice. He was instrumental in persuading Catherine to come to Harlem.

16. *Restoration: The Madonna House Newspaper* continues to be published today.

17. Merton included this letter to Catherine in his "Cold War Letters," a selection of letters Merton wrote between October 1961 and October 1962 on the topic of war and peace. Merton mimeographed and bound these letters for private distribution to friends.

18. Fr. Geno Baroni (1930–1984), a social activist who served as Assistant Housing Secretary under President Jimmy Carter. In the early 1960s he made a retreat at Madonna House in Ontario, Canada, an experience that had a profound influence on his later work.

19. In 1965, under pressure from Cardinal Francis Spellman of New York, Daniel Berrigan was sent to work in South America for a period of time.

20. On November 9, 1965, Roger La Porte, a Catholic worker, immolated himself on the steps of the United Nations building as a protest against the Vietnam War.

# SELECTED BIBLIOGRAPHY

Burden, Shirley. *God is My Life: The Story of Our Lady of Gethsemani.* Introduction by Thomas Merton. New York: Reynal, 1960.

Doherty, Catherine de Hueck. *Dear Bishop.* New York: Sheed and Ward, 1947.

———. *Dear Seminarian.* Milwaukee, WI: Bruce Publishing Company, 1950.

———. *Fragments of My Life.* Combermere, Ontario: Madonna House Publications, 1996.

———. *Friendship House.* New York: Sheed and Ward, 1946.

———. *My Russian Yesterdays.* Milwaukee, WI: Bruce Publishing Company, 1951.

———. *Not Without Parables.* Combermere, Ontario: Madonna House Publications, 1989.

———. *Poustinia: Christian Spirituality of the East for Western Man.* Notre Dame, IN: Ave Maria Press, 1975.

Duquin, Lorene Hanley. *They Called Her the Baroness: The Life of Catherine de Hueck Doherty.* New York: Alba House, 1995.

Merton, Thomas. *The Hidden Ground of Love: The Letters of Thomas Merton on Religious Experience and Social Concerns*. Edited by William H. Shannon. New York: Farrar, Straus & Giroux, 1985.

———. *Run to the Mountain*. Edited by Patrick Hart, O.C.S.O. Vol. 1 (1939–1941) of *The Journals of Thomas Merton*. HarperSanFrancisco, 1995.

———. *The Secular Journal of Thomas Merton*. New York: Farrar, Straus & Cudahy, 1959.

———. *The Seven Storey Mountain*. New York: Garden City Books, Garden City, 1951. First published 1948 by Harcourt, Brace.

———. *The Sign of Jonas*. New York: Harcourt, Brace, 1953.

———. *Thoughts in Solitude*. New York: Farrar, Straus & Cudahy, 1958.

Mott, Michael. *The Seven Mountains of Thomas Merton*. Boston: Houghton Mifflin Company, 1984.

Vishnewski, Stanley. *Wings of the Dawn*. New York: Catholic Worker, 1984.

Wild, Robert, ed. *Comrades Stumbling Along: The Friendship of Catherine de Hueck Doherty and Dorothy Day as Revealed through Their Letters*. Staten Island, NY: Alba House, 2009.

**Fr. Robert A. Wild** was ordained a priest for the Diocese of Buffalo in 1967, and for many years has lived in Madonna House, a community of laywomen, laymen, and priests founded by Catherine de Hueck Doherty. He is the author of several books, including a trilogy on Doherty's spirituality. Wild helped in editing a number of Doherty's writings, including *Poustinia*, and now serves as the postulator for her cause for canonization.

---

**Catherine de Hueck Doherty** (1896–1985) was born in Russia in 1896 and emigrated to Canada in 1921. In 1938 she established Friendship House in Harlem, New York—an interracial center that distributed goods to the poor and conducted lectures and discussion groups to promote racial understanding. After hearing her talk at St. Bonaventure University in 1941, Thomas Merton came to Harlem and the two became friends. Doherty later founded the Madonna House community in Combermere, Ontario. She lived there until her death in 1985, and her cause was opened in 1994. She has been given the title Servant of God.

**Thomas Merton** (1915–1968) is widely acclaimed as one of the most influential spiritual masters of the twentieth century. A monk, poet, spiritual writer, and social activist, he is perhaps best known for his spiritual autobiography, *The Seven Storey Mountain*.

Founded in 1865, Ave Maria Press,
a ministry of the Congregation of
Holy Cross, is a Catholic publishing
company that serves the spiritual and
formative needs of the Church and its
schools, institutions, and ministers;
Christian individuals and families; and
others seeking spiritual nourishment.

For a complete listing of titles from

Ave Maria Press

Sorin Books

Forest of Peace

Christian Classics

visit www.avemariapress.com

**ave maria press** / Notre Dame, IN 46556
A Ministry of the Indiana Province of Holy Cross